A 60 Second Lan

TALK
Nigeria

Teaches you how to communicate with
the majority of Nigerians
in 3 major common languages and their dialects
in less than a minute

YORUBA—IGBO–HAUSA

by: King Kayode Yeotan

Talk Nigeria
A Sixty-Second Language Handbook

iUniverse books may be ordered through booksellers or by contacting:

iUniverse
1663 Liberty Drive
Bloomington, IN 47403
www.iuniverse.com
1-800-Authors (1-800-288-4677)

ISBN: 978-1-4620-2006-5 (pbk)
ISBN: 978-1-4620-2007-2 (clth)
ISBN: 978-1-4620-2008-9 (ebk)

Library of Congress Control Number: 2011912579

Printed in the United States of America

iUniverse rev. date: 07/21/2011

Table of Contents

Introduction

Talk Nigeria is a language handbook that was designed to teach the Nigerian language in a very short period of time. This book will allow any English-speaking individual to quickly communicate in the three main languages: Yoruba, Igbo, & Hausa. For both native Nigerians and those that are interested in their languages, Talk Nigeria will offer the opportunity to correctly master the pronounciations of the native languages. This hand book will give you both the English translation for the Nigerian phrase or term, as well as the "English" pronounciation. For example, to phonetically pronounce the word "opportunity", you would break it down into five syllables as follows:

- "Opportunity"- **Awe-por-too-nee-tee**

Pronounce these words "phonetically" just as you would any other English term. Talk Nigeria is set up in this same format. Throughout this handbook, you will see the English phrase followed by the English pronounciation and the Yoruba term/ phrase.

Many other language books fail to provide a guideline for the correct pronounciations of the terms and phrases in other languages. Talk Nigeria focuses on this aspect and will have you speaking Nigerian in 60 seconds.

TALK NIGERIA

Nigerian Facts

Area: .... 923,766 sq.km.

Population: .... 150 million (estimate)

Capital: .... Abuja (9°4′N 7°29′E)

Government: ..... Three-tier structure:

- A Federal Government
- 36 StateGovernments
- 774 Local Government Administrations

Official Language: ... _English_

Main Indigenous Languages: ... Hausa, Igbo, Yoruba

Main Religions: ... Christianity, Islam, Traditional

Main Commercial/Industrial Cities: ...... Lagos, Onitsha, Kano, Ibadan, Port Harcourt, Aba, Maiduguri, Jos, Kaduna, Warri, Benin, Nnewi

Major Industrial Complexes:

Refineries and Petro-Chemicals: Kaduna, Warri, Port Harcourt, And Eleme.

Iron and Steel: Ajaokuta, Warri, Oshogbo, Katsina, Jos.

Fertilizer: Onne- Port Harcourt, Kaduna, Minna, Kano

Liquefied Natural Gas: Bonny

Aluminum Smelter: Ikot Abasi, Port Harcourt

Currency:

NAIRA and KOBO N1.00 = l00k
(one naira = hundred kobo)

Climate:

Temperatures across the country are relatively high with a very narrow variation in seasonal and diurnal ranges (22-36t). There are two basic seasons; wet season (April – October) and the dry season (November – March). The dry season commences with Harmattan, a dry chilly spell that lasts till February and is associated with lower temperatures, a dusty and hazy atmosphere brought about by the North-Easterly winds blowing from the Arabian peninsular across the Sahara. The second half of the dry season, February - March, is the hottest period of the year when temperatures range from 33 to 38°C. The extremes of the wet season are felt on the southeastern coast where annual rainfall might reach a high of 330cm. The extremes of the dry season, in aridity and high temperatures, are felt in the north third of the country.

Language History: NIGERIA

Nigeria has more than 250 ethnic groups, with varying languages and customs, creating a country of rich ethnic diversity. The largest ethnic groups are the <u>Fulani/Hausa</u>, <u>Yoruba</u>, and <u>Igbo</u>, accounting for 68% of population. The official language of Nigeria, English, was chosen to facilitate the cultural and linguistic unity of the country.

In Nigeria, there are three main Languages apart from english. The languages derived their names from the group of people they belong to.

1. **Yoruba** .... yo-roo-bah

2. **Ibo** (also spelled **Igbo**) ....he-boh

3. **Hausa** .... ha-oo-sah

- However, there are more than 300 dialects, within the three main languages and across them!

Yoruba

Yoruba language is one of the three official Languages of Nigeria. The Yoruba language is a dialect continuum of West Africa with over 22 million speakers.

The native tongue of the Yoruba people is spoken, among other languages, in Nigeria, Benin, and Togo. Traces of the language are also among communities in Brazil, Sierra Leone, where it is called Oku (oh-ku), and Cuba where it is called Nago (nah-go).

Nigeria was colonized by the British on October 1st 1960. To obtain the independence, the country's official language became English. A variation of English known as "broken English" or "Pidgin English" is also used.

Examples:

ENGLISH	PIDGIN ENGLISH	PRONUNCIATION
What	"Wetin"	way-teen
I'm going	"I de go"	ah-day-go
I would not go	"I no go go"	hi-no-go-go

Igbo

Igbo is the second of the three official languages of Nigeria and is a member of the Niger-Congo family of languages. The Igbo are the second largest group of people living in southern Nigeria. This language is spoken by about 18 million people in Nigeria and Equatorial Guinea. Igbo is a tonal language with two distinctive tones, high and low. In some cases a third, down stepped high tone is recognized. As of today, the Igbo language is not considered to be a full and complete language.

Hausa

Hausa is a Chadic language with about 39 million speakers. The Hausa people are mostly found in the southwestern parts of Niger and in the northwestern part of Nigeria called "Hausaland". About one-fourth of their language is derived from Arabic and the rest from Fulfulde and Kanuri languages, and even some English is incorporated into their language. Some Hausa even speak French and English fluently and sometimes even read and write Arabic. This language is also spoken in Niger, Benin, Burkina Faso, Cameroon, CAR, Chad, Congo, Eritrea, Germany, Ghana, Sudan and Togo.

YORUBA

Yoruba people are one of the largest ethnic groups in West Africa. The Yoruba language is spoken by majority of the Yoruba people. (Yoruba: *èdèe Yorùbá*; èdè). Throughout West Africa, the Yoruba are comprised of around 30 million individuals with approximately 21 percent of its total population predominantly found in Nigeria.

TALK NIGERIA

Yoruba Introduction

The traditional Yoruba area — currently comprising the southwestern portion of Nigeria, the republics of Benin and Togo — is commonly called **Ìlẹ-Yorùbá** (he-leh yoroo-bah) or Yorubaland.

Yoruba is a tonal language with three tones: high, mid, low!

The high tone is indicated by acute accent on top of letters (/).

The mid tones are not marked (-) and the low tones are marked with the grave acute on top of letter (\).

Yoruba Alphabet

LETTER	PRONOUNCIATION "SOUNDS LIKE"	LETTER
Aa	Ha	'Ahh' (hard a)
Bb	Bee	'Bee'
Dd	Dee	'Dee'
Ee	Hay-	'A'
Ẹẹ	Eh	'e' sound in 'let'
Ff	Fee	Fee
Gg	Gee	'g' sound in 'get'
Gb	G- bee	Gbee (hard g)
Hh	He— higher tone	'he'
Ii	He! - lower tone	'ee'
Jj	Jee	'g'
Kk	Kee	Key
Ll	Lee	Lee
Mm	Me	'Me'
Nn	Ne	Nee
Oo	Oh	O
Ọọ	Or	'au' as in 'fault'
Pp	Pee	P (heavy p)
Rr	Ree	Ree
Ss	See	See
Ṣṣ	She	She
Tt	Tee	Tea
Uu	Yu	'Oo' as in 'loose'
Ww	We	Wee
Yy	Ye	Yee

CARDINAL NUMBERS		PRONUNCIATION
1	Okan/eni	Hor-con
2	Meji	May-jee
3	Meta	Meh-tah
4	Merin	Meh-reen
5	Marun	Mah-roon
6	Mefa	Meh-fah
7	Meje	May-jay
8	Mejo	Meh-jaw
9	Mesan	Meh-son
10	Mewa	Meh-wah

ORDINAL NUMBERS		PRONUNCIATION
1st	Ekini	Hay-key-nee
2nd	Ekeji	Hay-kay-gee
3rd	Eketa	Eh-keh-tah
4th	Ekerin	Eh-keh rin
5th	Ekarun	Eh-kah-roon
6th	Ekefa	Eh-keh-fah
7th	Ekeje	Eh-keh jay
8th	Ekejo	Eh-keh jaw
9th	Ekesan	Eh-keh-son
10th	Ekewa	Eh-keh-wah

Yoruba Attire
Aso Ile Yoruba
(ah-shor-he-leh-wah)

YORUBA TERM	PRONUNCIATION	ENGLISH TRANSLATION
Buba	Boo-bah	-short loose garment terminating at the waist worn by both males and females
Iro	He-row	wrapper/ ceremonial skirt
Gele	Gay-lay	head tie/ head scarf
Sokoto	Sho-ko-to	native pant
Bante	Ban-teh	apron
Ipele	He-pay-lay	-smaller outer cloth worn by women
Fila	Fee-lah	cap or hat
Oja	Or-jah	band belt

Greetings Of Kings In Yoruba Language

Bi Ase Nki Oba Ni Ile Yoruba

(bee-ah-shay-n –kee- or-ba-nee-he-leh-yo-ru-bah)

YORUBA PHRASE	PRONUNCIATION	ENGLISH TRANSLATION
Ka-biye-si-o	car-bee-yea-see- oh	(same as) Long live the king
Oba alaye luwa	or-bar-ah-la-yea-loo-wah	(same as) Long live the king
Ki Ade ope lori	kee- ha-day-oh-peh-lo-ree	(same as) Long live the king
Ki bata ope lese	kee-bar-tah-oh peh –leh-seh	(same as) Long live the king

Greetings In Yoruba Language

Ikini Ni Ede Yoruba

YORUBA PHRASE	PRONUNCIATION	ENGLISH TRANSLATION
E KA RO	eh-car-raw	GOOD MORNING
E KA SAN	eh-car—son	GOOD AFTERNOON
E KA LE	eh-car-leh	GOOD EVENING
O DA RO	oh-dah-raw	GOOD NITE
BA WO NI KAN	bar-wo-nee-con	HOW ARE YOU
E KA BO	eh car-bor	WELCOME
O DA BO	oh-dah-bor	GOOD BYE
O SE (same age group or younger)	oh-shay	THANK YOU
E SE (someone older or addressing a group of people)	eh-shay	THANK YOU
E KU ISE	eh-coo-he-sheh	WELL DONE
SE ALAFIA NI E WA	shay –al-la-fee-ah—nee-eh-wah	ARE YOU OKAY
E PELE	eh-peh-leh	I AM SORRY
E MA BINU	eh ma-bee-nu	I APOLOGIZE
MO MO	mo-mor	I KNEW
MIO MO	me-oh-mor	I DON'T KNOW
BA WO NI	bar-wo-nee	WHATS UP
FI ARA BALE	far-rah-bar-leh	TAKE IT EASY
E WO LO NSE LE	hay-woe- lone-cher-leh	WHATS GOIN ON

Phrases You Should Know

YORUBA PHRASE	PRONUNCIATION	ENGLISH TRANSLATION
E LO NI	Hay-lo-nee	HOW MUCH
ME LO NI	May-lo-nee	HOW MANY
MO FE	Mo-feh	I NEED
SE ONI	Shay-oh-nee	DO YOU HAVE
MO FE	Mo-feh	I WANT
MO NI	Mo-nee	I HAVE
MIO NI	Me-oh-nee	I DON'T HAVE
MO MO	Mo- mor	I KNOW
E SE	Eh-shay	THANK YOU
A KO NI KANKAN	Ha-co-nee con-con	WE DON'T HAVE ANY
NI BO	Nee-bo	WHERE IS
KILO FE	Kee-lo-feh	WHAT DO YOU WANT
MIO MO	Mee-oh-mor	I DON'T KNOW
INU MI DUN	He-nu-me-doon	I AM HAPPY
SE ENI	Shay-eh-nee	DO YOU HAVE
EYI NI	Hay-yee-nee	THIS IS
NIBO NI	Nee-bo-nee	WHERE ARE
O DA BE	Oh-dah-beh	IT'S ALRIGHT
MO TI SE TAN	Mo-tee-shay-ton	I AM FINISHED
MO TIN LO	Mo-teen-law	I AM GOING
MO NBO	Moan-boh	I AM COMING
JE KA LO	Jeh-car-lor	LET'S GO
WA NBI	Wan- bee	COME HERE
MA PE E	Ma-pay-eh	I WILL CALL YOU
E MI NI	Hay- me-nee	JUST ME

SE OWA DADA	Shay-oh-wa-dah-da	ARE YOU OKAY
DIDE	Dee-day	GET UP
JOKO	Joh-ko	Sit down
BO YA	Bo-yah	Maybe
MO TI SESE	Mo-tee-shay-shay	I am hurt
OWO MI DA	Oh-wo-me-dah	Where is my money
NIBO LOWA	Nee-boh-lo-wah	Where are you
NIBO LON LO	Nee-boh-lone-lor	Where are you going
KILO FE JE	Kilo-feh-jeh	What do you want to eat
KILO FE MU	Kilo-feh-moo	What do you want to drink
KILO FE SE	Kilo-feh-shay	What do you want to do
KILO FE RA	Kilo-feh-rah	What do you want to buy
KILO FE TA	Kilo-feh-tah	What do you want to sell

A Short List of Trees

YORUBA TERM	PRONUNCIATION	ENGLISH TRANSLATION
ABAFE	ah-ba-feh	BAUHINIA RETICULATA
ABIDUN	ah-bee- doon	KOLA
ABO	ah-boh	CUSTARD APPLE
ABO IDOFUN	ah- boh- he- door-foon	PARANARIUMCURATE LLAE-FOLIUM
ABO-LAKOSHE	ah-boh-lah-ko-shay	CALABASH NUTMEG
AFARA	ah-fah-rah	SHINGLE WOOD
AFE	ah- feh	ALLIGATOR APPLE
AFON	ah-forn	AFRICAN BREAD FRUIT
AGA	ah- gah	CORK WOOD, OR UMBRELLA
AGA-IGI	ah-gah-he-gee (gee as geek)	LIGHT AFRICAN GREEN HEART
AGBA	hag-ba	CLITANDRA TOYOLANA
AGBON OLODU	hag-bon —oh-lo-du	AFRICAN FAN-PALM (PALMYRA PALM)
AHUN	ah-hoon	WHITE WOOD
AJAGBON	ah jarg-born	INDIAN TAMARIND(INDIA DATE)
AKO	ah-ko	IRON WOOD
AKO EJIRIN	ah-cor—hay-jee-reen	AFRICAN CUCUMBER
AKO-IRE	ah-cor-he-ray	SPURIOUS RUBBER TREE

Yoruba Reference Dictionary

ENGLISH	YORUBA TERM	PRONUNCIATION
A		
ABANDON	kor-see-leh	KO-SILE
ABBEY	he-lay-or-lor-roon	ILE-OLORUN
ABDOMEN	he- koon	IKUN
ABIDE	bah jo-ko	BA-JOKO
ABILITY	oh-ye	OYE
ABROAD	he-dah-leh	IDALE
ACADEMY	he-lay-eh-cor	ILE-EKO
ACCESS	or-non	ONA
ACCIDENT	jam-bah	JAMBA
ACCOMPLISH	he-shea-parry	ISE PARI
ACCORD	or-con-con	OKAN-KAN
ACTIVITY	he-ya-rah	IYARA
ACTUAL	nee-toe-toe	NITOTO
ADORATION	he-yeen-lo-go	IYIN-LOGO
ADORE	ju-bah	JUBA
ADVERSARY	or-tah	OTA
ADVICE	he-mor-run	IMORAN
AFRAID	beh-roo	BERU
AFRESH	ne-toon-toon	NI TUNTUN
AGAIN	leh-kay-gee	LEKEJI
AGAINST	doe- ju- cor	DOJUKO
AGE	or-jaw-ho-ree	OJO ORI
AGREEMENT	ha-day-hoon	ADEHUN

AIR	ha-feh-feh	AFEFE
ALCOHOL	or-tee-lee-lay	OTI LILE
ALIAS	ho-ru--cor-me-run	ORUKO-MIRAN
ALIKE	bar-con-nor	BAKANA
AND	ah-tee	ATI
ANGEL	han-geh-lee	ANGELI
ANGER	he--be-nu	IBINU
ANIMAL	eh-run-co	ERAN KO
ANIMOSITY	he-bee-nu	IBINU
ANKLE	co-co-seh	KOKOSE
ANNIVERSARY	aj-jaw-doon	AJODUN
ANNOUNCE	kay-day	KEDE
ANNOINT	toh-row-roh-see	TOROROSI
ANOTHER	o-me-ron	OMIRAN
ANYBODY	en-nee keh-nee	ENIKENI
ANYONE	hay-ye-kay-yee	EYIKEYI
APOLOGY	eh-beh	EBE
ARISE	dee-day	DI DE
AVOID	yeh-rah-foon	YE-RA FUN
B		
BABY	or-mor-wor	OMO OWO
BACK	eh-yeen	EHIN
BAD	boo-roo	BURU
BATTLE	he-jah	IJA
BEAD	he-leh-keh	ILEKE
BEAN	eh-wah	EWA
BEWARE	shaw-rah	SORA
BIG	toe-bee	TOBI

BIRD	eh-yeh	EIYE
BIRTHDAY	or-jor-he-be	OJO IBI
BLACK	du-du	DUDU
BLANK	sho-foe	SOFO
BOMB	ah-fon-jah	AFONJA
BOW	teh-re-bah	TERIBA
BRIDE	he-ye-wo	IYAWO
BROOM	or-war	OWO
BURIAL	he-seen-ku	ISINKU
BUSH	hig-bow	IGBO
C		
CALL	pay	PE
CAMEL	rah-coom-me	RAKUNMI
CANOE	or-kor	OKO
CAPITALIST	oh-low-woe	OLOWO
CAPTAIN	or-ga-goon	OGAGUN
CASAVA	eh-geh	EGE
CASE	eh-jor	EJO
CASH	owe-woe	OWO
CASHEW	ka-ju	KAJU
CAT	ho-loh-g-boh	OLOGBO
CAUSE	he-dee	IDI
CELEBRITY	he-ya-rah	IYARA
CEMENT	ha-mor-le-lay	AMO-LILE
CHILD	or-mor-day	OMODE
CINDER	hay—du	EDU
CLEVER	mo-yea	MOYE
COME	wah	WA
COMPLAINT	eh-jor	ESUN,EJO
COWARD	or-leh	OJO,OLE

CRAB	ah-con	AKAN
CROWN	ah-day	ADE
CRY	eh-coon	EKUN
CURVE	ko-doh-roe	KODORO
CUTLASS	ah-dah	ADA
CYNIC	a-la-roe-roe	ALARORO
D		
DAILY	o-joh-ju-moh	OJOJUMO
DANCE	joe	JO
DEFECT	a-boo-ku	ABUKU
DEMON	hay-shu	ESU
DESTINY	ha-yarn-mor	AYANMO
DIFFERENT	ya-tore	YATO
DISCUSS	wah-dee	WADI
DISGRACE	he-tee-joo	ITIJU
DISTANT	gee-nah	JINA
DIVORCE	kaw-see-leh	KO SILE
DOG	ah-jah	AJA
DREAM	ah-la	ALA
DRUM	he-loo	ILU
DUMPY	ku-ku-roo	KUKURU
E		
EACH	or-con-con	OKANKAN
EASE	he-ro-rah	IRORA
EAT	jeh-oon	JEUN
EGG	eh-yeen	EYIN
ELBOW	he-goon-pa	IGUNPA
ENEMY	or-tah	OTA
END	o-pin	OPIN
ENGINE	eh-raw	ERO

EQUIP	shay-law-shore	SE LOSO
EYE	o-joo	OJU
EYE WITNESS	eh-leh-re	ELERI
F		
FACE	o-joo	OJU
FACT	o-te-taw	OTITO
FALL	shu-boo	SUBU
FAME	o-kee-kee	OKIKI
FAMILY	e-bee	EBI
FARINA	ga-ree	GARI
FATHER	bah-bah	BABA
FEAR	eh-roo	ERU
FELL	shubu	SUBU
FEMALE	oh-be-reen	OBINRIN
FEVER	he-bar	IBA
FIANCEE	ha-feh-saw-nor	AFESONA
FIGHT	jah	JA
FIND	wah	WA
FLAVOUR	ha-doon	ADUN
FOLLY	way-ray	IWERE
FOOD	own-jeh	ONJE
FOX	kolo-kolo	KOLOKOLO
FRAUD	eh-ton	ETAN
G		
GATE	eh-nu-or-nor	ENU-ONA
GHOST	ho-coo	OKU
GIFT	eh-boon	EBUN
GIRL	or-mor-ho-be-reen	OMO OBIRIN
GLAD	yor	YO

GREED	ha-woon	AWUN
GRIEF	eh-doon	EDUN
GUARD	ah-bo	ABO
GUILT	eh-she	ESE
GUN	he-bon	IBON
H		
HAIR	he-roon	IRUN
HAND	oh-wo	OWO
HAPPY	la-lah-fia	LALAFIA
HABOUR	hay-boo-tay	EBUTE
HARMFUL	nee-pah-lah-ra	NIPALARA
HATE	ko-re-rah	KORIRA
HAUL	far	FA
HAWK	ha-wo-dee	AWODI
HEAD	ho-ree	ORI
HEAL	wo-son	WO SAN
HEART	or-con	OKAN
HEAT	ho-roo	ORU
HELL	hor-roon ha-pa-dee	ORUN APADI
HERO	ha-ko-ni	AKONI
I		
ICE	owe-mee-dee-dee	OMI DIDI
IDOL	ho-re-sha	ORISA
IGNORANT	la-he-mor	LAIMO
IGNORE	fe-oh-ju-fo-dah	FI OJU FODA
ILLEGAL	low-dee-see-oh-fin	LODI SI OFIN
IMAGE	hay-ray	ERE

IMAGINE	ro	RO
IMITATE	teh-lay	TELE
IMMORAL	boo-roo	BURU
IMMORTAL	lah--e—coo	LAIKU
IMPEACH	peh-leh-hoe	PE-LEJO
IMPRISON	ha-mor	HA-MO
INJURY	he-fa-rah-pah	IFARAPA
IVORY	Eh-reen eh-reen	EHIN ERIN
J		
JAIL	eh-won	EWON
JAW	ag-bon	AGBON
JEALOUS	ho-woo	OWU
JEST	eh-feh	EFE, AWADA
JESUS	jay-su	JESU
JIGGER	gee-ga	JIGA
JOKE	a-pa-rah	APARA
JOY	a-yuh	AYO
JUSTICE	ho-tee-tor	OTITO
JUSTIFY	da-lah-ray	DA LARE
K		
KEEL	or-kor	ISAKE, OKO
KEEPPER	oh-lu-pa-mor	OLUPAMO,ONITOJU
KICK	tar-pa	TAPA,
KID	or-mor-hay-wu-reh	OMO EWURE
KIDNAP	gee-gbay	JI GBE
KILL	par	PA
KIN	he-bar-ton	IBATAN
KIND	or-war	OWO
KING	or-bah	OBA

KINGDOM	he-jor-bah	IJOBA
KINGSHIP	oh-yea-or-bah	OYE OBA
KINGSMAN	he-bar-ton -- or-koon-reen	IBATAN OKUNRIN
KINSWOMAN	he-bar-ton--- oh-be-reen	IBATAN OBINRIN
KISS	feh-nu-keh-nu	IFENU KENU
KITCHEN	he-be-dah-nor	IBI IDANA
KITTEN	or-mor -ho-lo-gbo	OMO OLOGBO
KNEE	eh-koon	EKUN
KNEEL	koon-leh	KUNLE
KNELL	he-row-ah-go-go	IRO OGOGO
KNIFE	or-beh	OBE
KNOB	ko-ko	KOKO
KNOW	mor	MO
KNOWING	mo-yea	GBON,MOYE
KNOWINLY	mor-mor	MOMO
KNOWLEDGE	he-mor	IMO
KOLA	o-bee	OBI
L		
LABEL	he-way-sa-me	IWE SAMI
LABOUR	he-cher	ISE
LACK	ha-he-nee	AINI
LAD	or-mor koon-reen	OMOOKUNRIN
LADDER	ha-ka-ba	AKABA
LADY	or-mor-gay	OMOGE
LAND	he-leh	ILE
LAMB	ha-goon-ton	AGUNTAN

LAME	ha-mu-kun	AMUNKUN
LAMP	ha-tu-pah	ATUPA
LAMPLIGHT	he-mor-leh	IMOLE
LANDLADY/LANDLORD	oh-ne-lay	ONILE
LATE	ho-peh	OPE
LATER	le-hin-na	LEHIN NA
LAUGH	reh-reen	RERIN
LAVISH	he-non-koo-non	INAKUNA
LAW	oh-feen	OFIN
LAW BREAKER	ah-roo-feen	ARUFIN
LAW GIVER	ah-sho-feen	ASOFIN
LAZY	or-leh	OLE
LEAD	o-jay	OJE
LEADER	ah-she-wa-ju	ASIWAJU
LEAF	ay-way	EWE
LEAK	jo	JO
LEARN	kor-eh-kor	KO EKO
LEG	eh-she	ESE
LEMON	or-rum-baw key-con	OROMBO,KIKAN
LEOPARD	eh-koon	EKUN
LEPER	ah-deh-the	ADETE
LEPROSY	eh-the	ETE
LESS	kay-ray-ju	KEREJU
LIAR	oh-pu-raw	OPURO
LIGHTLY	jeh-jeh	JEJE
LION	ke-ne-hoon	KINIUN
LITTLE	kay-ray	KERE

LIVER	eh-dor	EDO
LOAD	er-roo	ERU
LOCK SMITH	ah-la-gbe-deh	ALAGBEDE
LOOK	woe	WO
LORD	oh-lu-wah	OLUWA
LOST	sor-nu	SONU
LOT	he-pow	IPO
LOVE	he-feh	IFE
LOVER	ho-loo-feh	OLUFE
LOYAL	ho-lo-tor	OLOTO
LUCIFER	hay-shu	ESU
LYING	ho-pu-raw	OPURO
M		
MACHINE	eh-raw	ERO
MAD	she -way-ray	SIWERE
MAGIC	he-don	IDAN
MAKER	eh-leh-dar	ELEDA
MALARIA	ah-kor-he-bah	AKO IBA
MALE	ar-kor	AKO
MANGER	he-bu-jeh-ron	IBUJE ERAN
MANY	pu-por	PUPO
MEN	or-koon-reen	OKONRIN
MENTION	ron-tee	IRANTI
MERRY	lah-yor	LAYO
MET	pa-day	PADE
MINE	tay-me	TEMI
MODEL	ah-peh-reh	APERE,
MONEY	oh-wo	OWO
MONKEY	or-bor	OBO,LAGIDO
MOOD	he-wah	IWA

MOON	oh-shu-pah	OSUPA
MOPE	fo-ju-ro	FAJURO
MORROW	or-la	OLA
MORSEL	o-kay-lay	OKELE
MOSLEM	he-ma-lay	IMALE
MOSQUE	mor-sha-la-she	MOSALASI
MOSQUITO	eh-forn	EFON
MOTHER	he-ya	IYA
MOTHER IN LAW	he-ya-or-kaw- or (he ya-woe)	IYA OKO , IYA IYAWO
MYTHOLOGY	he-jar-raw	IJARO
N		
NAG	yor-leh-nu	YO-LENU
NAKED	he-ho-ho	NIHOHO
NAME	ho-ru-kor	ORUKO
NAP	to-g-bay	TOGBE
NARROW	torow	TORO
NATIONALITY	ha-ra-he-lu	ARAILU
NATIVE	he-bee-leh	IBILE
NEAR	ne-to-see	NITOSI
NECK	or-roon	ORUN
NECKLACE	he-leh-keh- or-roon	ILEKE ORUN
NEGOTIATE	ha-day-hun	ADEHUN
NEGRO	doo-doo	DUDU
NET	ha-won	AWON
NEVER	lah-he	LAI
NEW	tee-toon	TITUN
NO	ho-tee	OTI
NUDE	ne-ho-ho	NIHOHO

O		
OAK	he-gee as geek	IGI OAKU
OATH	he-boo-rah	IBURA
OBIDIENT	fo-ree-bah-leh	IFORIBALE
OBSERVE	ha-kee-yeea-see	AKIYESI
OCEAN	ho-koon un-lah	OKUN NLA
ONION	ha-loo-bor-sa	ALUBOSA
ONLY	pay-ray	PERE
OPEN	she	SI
ORACLE	or-raw-he-gin-leh	ORO IJINLE
ORGAN	doo-roo	DURU
ORGANIST	ah-teh-doo-roo	ATE-DURU
OWE	jeh-oh-wo	JE NI GBESE
OWL	oh-we-we	OWIWI
OWNER	oh-lo-hun	OLOHUN
OX	ma-loo	MALU
P		
PAD	ho-shu-ka	OSUKA
PADDLE	he-wa-leh	IWALE
PAGAN	ha-bo-ree-sha	ABORISA
PALM OIL	hay-poe	EPO
PALM WINE	eh-mu	EMU
PANIC	he-pah-yah	IPAIYA
PAPA	bah-bah	BABA
PARRALLEL,	eh-jor-rah	IJORA
PARCEL	eh-roo	ERU
PARDON	he-dah-ree-jee	IDARIJI

PASSENGER	hay-roe	ERO
PASSING	kor-ja-lor	NKOJA LO
PASSION	he-tah-rah	ITARA
PAWPAW	he-beh-peh	IBEPE
PAY	son-ho-wo	SAN OWO
PEACE	ha-la-fear	ALAFIA
PEEL	bow	BO
PENALTY	he-gee-yah	IYA,IJIYA
PEOPLE	hay -ne-yon	ENIA
PERIOD	ho-pin	OPIN
PEST	ha-roon	ARUN
PIG	eh-leh-deh	ELEDE
PIONEER	ha-she-wa-ju	ASAJU
PITY	ha-nu	ANU
PLACE	he-pow	IBI,IPO
POLE	oh-poe	OPO
PRAY	bah-doo-rah	GBADURA
PRIDE	hig-bay-rah-ga	IGBERAGA
PRIVILEGE	an-fa-nee	ANFANI
PROFIT	hay-ray	ERE
PSALM	ho-reen-me-mor	ORIN MIMO
PUMKIN	hay-lay-gay-day	ELEGEDE
PURSE	ha-poe	APO
PUS	or-yunn	OYUN
PUT	fe-see	FISI
PYTHON	oh jho-la	OJOLA
Q		
QUAIL	beh-roo	BERU

QUAINT	ha-jay-gee	AJEJI
QUAY	hay-boo-tay	EBUTE
QUEEN	ho-lo-ree	OLOREE
QUEST	he-wa-kee-ree	IWAKIRI
QUICK	yah-rah	YARA
QUICKLY	kee-ah-kee-ah	KIAKIA
QUILT	he-bo-ree	IBORI
QUOTH	wee-pay	WIPE
R		
RABBIT	hay-ho-roe	EHORO
RACE	he-ru	IRU
RACKET	ha-ree-wo	ARIWO
RADIANCE	he-don	IDAN
RAGE	he-bee-noo	IBINU
RAIDER	ho-nee-jah-dee	ONIJADI
RAIN	oh-jo	OJO
RAINBOW	ho-shu-ma-ray	OSUMARE
RAM	ag-boe	AGBO
RAMADAN	ho-shu -ha-weh	OSU AWE IMALE
RANDOM	he-she-roe	ISIRO
RANK	he-pow	IPO
RAT	hay-coo-tay	EKUTE
RATE	he-yea	IYE
RECESS	ha-koe-koe	AKOKO
RECIPE	ha-pay-ju-we	APEJUWE
RECOLLECT	ron-tee	RANTI
REVEAL	fee-han	FIHAN
ROOM	yah-rah	YARA
ROUND	ro-bo-tow	ROBOTO
RUST	he-do-goon	IDOGUN

S		
SAD	fa-ju-row	FAJURO
SAME	he-kan-non	IKANNA
SAFE	lah-lah-fe-ha	LALAFIA
SALE	tah-or-jah	TA OJA
SAVAGE	hay-nee-yan--boo-roo-koo	ENIA BURUKU
SCHOOL	he-lay-he-way	ILE IWE
SCREEN	ah-bo	ABO
SECRET	ah-bo	ABO
SENIOR	ah-sha-ju	ASAJU
SENSELESS	lah-he-ne-mor	LAINIMO
SERMON	he-wah-su	IWASU
SHEEP	ah-goon-ton	AGUTAN
SHOE	bah-tah	BATA
SHORT	koo-roo	KURU
SHOUT	ah-ree-woe	ARIWO
SHRINE	ho-ree-sha	ORISA
SMALL	kay-kay-ray	KEKERE
SON	or-mor awe-koon-reen	OMO OKUNRIN
STAY	du-row	DA DURO
SWEET	dee-doon	DIDUN
SWORD	he-dah	IDA
SYSTEM	hay-row	ERO
T		
TABLE	tah-bee-lee	TABILI
TALE	he-ton	ITAN
TAKE	moo	MU
TALL	gee-gah	GIGA

TALLY	shay-day-day	SEDEDE
TARGET	ar-me	AMI
TEACH	eh-cor	EKO
TEST	he-don-woe	IDANWO
THAT	hay-ye	EYI
THANKS	he-doo-peh	IDUPE
THEOLOGY	he-mor-or-lor-roon	IMO OLORUN
THEORY	he-mor-he-dar-mor –ron	IMO,IDAMORAN
THESE	he-won-ye	IWONYI
THEY	ah-won	AWON
THIEF	oh-lay	OLE
THIGH	he-ton	ITAN
TIDY	he-mor-to-to	IMOTOTO
TIGER	ah-mor-the-koon	OMOTEKUN
TIME	ah-co-co	AKOKO
TITLE	o-yea	OYE
TODAY	lo-nee	LONI
TONE	he-row	IRO
TOO	poh-joo	POJU
TRAVEL	he-reen-ha-jo	IRIN AJO
TRUTH	ho-tee-tor	OTITO
TURKEY	tolo-tolo	TOLO TOLO
TWIN	he-bay-gee	IBEJI
TYPE	ha-peh-reh	APERE
U		
UDDER	or-mu-eh-ran-ko	OMU ERANKO
UGLY	la-he-leh-wah	LAILEWA

UNBRELLA	ag-boh-roon	AGBORUN
UNCUT	la-he-sha	LAISA
UNOFORMITY	bar-kon-nan	BAKANNA
UNWELL	sha-he-son	SAISAN
UTTERLY	pah-tah-pah-tah	PATAPATA
V		
VACANCY	ha-yea	AYE
VAGABOND	ah-lah-reen-kee-ree	ALA RINKIRI
VAGINA	o-boh	OBO
VANISH	sa-lor	SALO
VARIETY	oh-nee-roo-roo	ONIRURU
VELOCITY	he-ya-rah	IYARA
VENDOR	or-lor-jah	OLOJA
VERY	gon	GAN,PAPA
VICTOR	ah-she-goon	ASEGUN
VILLAGE	ha-boo-lay	ABULE
VIOLENT	he-cah	IKA
VOCATION	he-pay	ISE,IPE
W		
WAGE	ge-yon	JIYAN,SE ADEHUN
WAGON	keh-keh-roo	KEKE ERU
WAIF	ha-lah-he-nee he-leh	ALAINI ILE
WALK	reen	RIN
WALKER	ha-reen-non	ARINNA
WAN	joh-roh	JORO
WAND	ah-jay	AJE
WARRIOR	ho-lo-goon	OLOGUN

WARY	ne-sho-rah	NISORA
WASTE	sho-foh	FI SOFO
WATER	oh-me	OMI
WEED	hay-way	EWE
WELL	kon-gah	KANGA
WET	tu-tu	TUTU
WHEREVER	nee-bee-kee-bee	NIBIKIBI
WHICH	hay-woe	EWO
WHITE	foon-foon	FUNFUN
WHOLE	g-boh-g-boh	GBOGBO
WHY	kee-nee	KINI
WIRE	ho-koon-he-reen	OKUN IRIN
WISDOM	he-mor	IMO
WIZARD	ah-jeh	AJE
WOMAN	oh-bee-reen	OBINRIN
WOMB	he-nu	INU
WORRY	wah-ha-lah	WAHALA
WRONG	ah-she-shay	ASISE
Y		
YAM	he-shu	ISU
YE	on-yeen	ONYIN
YEAR	or-doon	ODUN
YEOMAN	or-mor-oh-goon	OMO OGUN
YES	beh-nee	BENI
YOU	he-wor	IWO
YOUTH	or-dor-mor-day	ODOMODE

Z		
ZEAL	he-tah-rah	ITARA
ZEBRA	keh-teh-keh-the	KETEKETE ABILA
ZERO	ho-foe	OFO
ZIGZAG	shay-gay-shay-gay	SEGE SEGE

TALK NIGERIA

IGBO

Igbo people are an ethnic group living chiefly in southeastern Nigeria. Today, a majority of them speak English alongside Igbo as a result of British colonialism. Igbo people are one of the largest and most influential ethnic groups in Nigeria.

TALK NIGERIA

Igbo
Language and Alphabet
The Igbo alphabet consist of 36 letters

LETTERS	PRONUNCIATION (SIMILAR SOUND IN ENGLISH WORDS)
A	'ah' as in annual, apple
B	'bee' as in become, behave
Ch	'ch' as in chalk, chapel
D	'dee' as in deed, dig, diego
E	'eh' as in egg, effort
F	'fee' as in field, fish
G	'geh' as in English word "get"
Gb	'beh' – hard sounding "b" as in fargboo
Gh	Sounds like neighbor, ghetto, cough
Gw	Sounds like gwent, quash
H	English word "he, hen, hair, hear"
I	'ee' as in either, ear, eaglet
Ịị	'i' sound in English word "ink"
J	Sounds like jail, jam, jack
K	English word "key"
Kp	Sounds like repute, catapult
Kw	Sounds like quote, quick, question
L	English word "lee"
M	English word "me"
N	English word no, note
Ňň	English nasal sound 'n' as in rung, gong, song
Nw	Sounds like went, wench, wept

Ny	Sounds like po**ny**, fun**ny**
O	English letter "o"
Ọọ	'au' as in English word "f**au**lt, **au**gment"
P	hard sounding "p" as in **p**ay, **p**ocket
R	're' as in **re**port, **re**produce, **re**search
S	English word "**s**ee"
Sh	English word "she" as in **sh**ip, **s**ure, **sh**all
T	English word "**t**ea"
U	'oo' as in English word "l**oo**se"
Ụụ	As in t**a**lk, p**o**rk, r**o**ck
V	English letter "v"
W	English word "**w**elt"
Y	Sounds like **y**ear, **y**ell, **y**east
Z	Sounds like **z**ero, **z**oo, **z**one

Igbo Numbers

NUMBER		PRONUNCIATION
1	**Otu**	oh-too
2	**Abuo**	ha-boo-oh
3	**Ato**	Hat-or
4	**Ano**	ha-nor
5	**Ise**	He-seh
6	**Isii**	He-see
7	**Asaa**	ha-sa
8	**Asato**	ah-sah-tow
9	**Itoolu**	He-too-ol-loo
10	**Iri**	He-ree

Common Phrases

ENGLISH	PRONUNCIATION	IGBO TRANSLATION
I WANT	ha-chom	ACHOM
WHERE ARE YOU?	kay-doo hey-bay he-no	KEDU EBE INO
WHAT ARE YOU DOING?	kay-doo he-hay he-nah m-eh	KEDU IHE INA EME
TAKE YOUR MONEY	way-ray hay-go gee	WERE EGO GI
I DON'T KNOW	ha-nee-ah-gym	ANIAGHIM
LEAVE ME ALONE	rap-oom ah-kah	RAPU M AKA
GOOD MORNING	he-boh-lah chee	IBOLA CHI
GOOD NIGHT	car chee fo	KA CHI FO
GOOD BYE	kor-dee	KODI
WELCOME	un-naw	NNOO
THANK YOU	dah-loo	DALU

Greetings in Igbo Language

ENGLISH PHRASE	PRONUNCIATION	IGBO TRANSLATION
GOOD MORNING	he- sa-lah-chi	EZIGBO UTUTU (ISALA CHI)
GOOD DAY	hu-bo-see-oh-ma	EZIGBO UBOSI (UBOSI OMA)
GOOD AFTERNOON	he –meh-lah---eh-fe-fay	EZIGBO EFIFE (IMELA EFIFE)
GOOD EVENING	hay-zig-bo—hum-be-deh	EZIGBO MGBEDE
GOOD NIGHT	han-yah-see---omah	EZIGBO ANYASI (ANYASI OMA)
HELLO	Kay-doo	KEDU
WELCOME	hun-nor	NNO
HOW ARE YOU	kay-doo kah o-dee	KEDU KA ODI?
I AM FINE	or-dean-mar	ODI MMA
THANK YOU	dah-loo	DALU
GOODBYE	kah-oh-dee	KA OMESIA(KA ODI)
LONG TIME NO SEE	ho-tay-kwana	OTE KWANA
PLEASE	bee- ko	BIKO
YES	Hay	EH
NO	Hum-bah	MBA
SORRY	In-doh	NDO
EXCUSE ME	Chay-reh-too	CHERETU
WHO?	Own-yeh	ONYE
WHAT?	o-gee-nee	OGINI
WHERE?	Eh-bee	EBEE
WHEN?	m-bay oh-lay	MGBE OLE
WHY?	O boo ah-kah gee-nee	O BU AKA GINI

HOW FAR?	Oh teh-ren awn-yah	O TERE ANYA
HOW MUCH?	Oh boo eh-go o-lay	O BU EGO OLE
WHAT IS THAT?	Oh-boo-gee-nee	O BU GINI
WHERE IS...?	Eh-bee kah	EBEE KA
I LIKE/ WANT	Ho-mah-see-reem	O MASIRI M
I DON'T LIKE/ WANT	Ho-mah-sig-him	O MASIGHI M
I KNOW	Ho-ma-m	A MA M
I DON'T KNOW	Ho-mig-m	A MAGHI M
DO YOU UNDERSTAND?	He-go-tah-rah	I GHOTARA
I UNDERSTAND	He-go-ta-tah-ram	A GHOTARA M
I DON'T UNDERSTAND	Ha-go-tag-him	A GHOTAGHI M
IS EVERYTHING OK?	He-hay nee-lay 0-deem-mah	IHE NILE O DIM MA

Igbo
Reference Dictionary

ENGLISH TERM	PRONUNCIATION	IGBO TERM
A		
ABANDON	hun-lo-zo	NLOZO
ABBEY	hun-no hun-sor	UNO NSO
ABDOMEN	ha-for	AFO
ABIDE	non-yeh-reh	NONYERE
ABILITY	he-keh	IKE
ABROAD	hor-feh-see	OFESI
ACADEMY	hun-no haku-kor dee eh-loo	UNO AKWUKWO DI ELU
ACCESS	hor-geh-reh	OGHERE
ACCIDENT	he-heh-mbeh-reh-deh	IHEMBEREDU
ACCOMPLISH	he-may-zoo	IMEZU
ACCORD	ho-too ho-bee	OTU OBI
ACTIVITY	hoe-lu	OLU
ACTUAL	hay-zee-hay	EZIE
ADORATION	ho-foo-feh	OFUFE
ADORE	ho-foo-feh	OFUFE
ADVERSARY	own-yeh he-lo	ONYE ILO
ADVICE	or-du	ODU
AFRAID	hu-jaw	UJO
AFRESH	hun-bee-daw	NBIDO
AGAIN	aw-zor	OZO
AGAINST	hum-may-ge-dah	NMEGIDE
AGE	ha-for	UFO
AGREEMENT	hin-pay-bee	NKPEBI
AIR	he-coo-coo	IKUKU
ALCOHOL	hun-man-yah	NMANYA

ALIAS	hana-por kwah	ANAKPO KWA
ALIKE	ho-too	OTU
AND	nah	NA
ANGEL	mon-sor	NMO NSO
ANGER	he-way	IWE
ANIMAL	ha-nu ho-fear	ANU OHIA
ANIMOSITY	ha-see	ASI
ANKLE	hor-ku oo-kwu	OKU UKWU
ANNIVERSARY	he-moo may-lota	E MIU ME LOTA
ANNOUNCE	he-may hawk-wah	IMA OKWA
ANNOINT	he-teh he- mah-noo	ITE NMANU
ANOTHER	hor-zor	OZO
ANYBODY	mah-doo hor-boo-nah	NMADU OBUNA
ANYONE	hor-yea hor-boo-nah	ONYE OBUNA
APOLOGY	hum-bah-rah	NGBAGHARA
ARISE	hum-may-nee-tay	NMANITE
AVOID	he-zeh-reh	IZERE
B		
BABY	hor-beh-ray wah	OBERE NWA
BACK	ha-zoo	AZU
BAD	ha-jaw	AJO
BATTLE	hor-goo	OGU
BEAD	gee-gee-dah	JIGIDA
BEAN	hag-wah	NKPULU AGWA
BEWARE	nee-heh ha-ka na-yan	NIE AKA NANYA
BIG	hu-nu-ku	NNUKWU
BIRD	hun-nor-nor	NNUNU
BIRTHDAY	u-bor-chi ho-mu-mu	UBECHI ONUMU
BLACK	oh-gee	OJI
BLANK	ho-po-koh-low	OKPOKOLO
BOMB	o-gu nah he-gway	OGBU NA IGWE
BOW	he-say-poo ha-na	ISEKPU ANA
BRIDE	hun-wan-yee or-fu	NWANYI OFU

BROOM	ha-zee-zah	AZIZA
BURIAL	heek-wah or-zoo	IKWA OZU
BUSH	ho-he-ha	OHIA
C		
CALL	ho-coo	OKU
CAMEL	he-yeen yah	INYI NYA
CANOE	hug-bor	UGBO
CAPTAIN	haw-chi-ha-ga	OCHIAGHA
CASAVA	ha-poo	AKPU
CASE	hak-pa	AKPA
CASH	hay-go	EGO
CAUSE	he-hay pah-tah-loo	IHE KPATALU
CELEBRITY	hor-see-saw	OSISO
CEMENT	un-too hah-loo hu-nor	NTU EJI ALU UNO
CINDER	hin-too nah hu-yee	NTU NA UNYI
CLEVER	he-dee kaw	IDI-NKO
COME	bee-ha	BIA
COMPLAINT	hun-peh-sah	NKPESA
COWARD	hon-yay hu-jaw	ONYE UJO
CRAB	she-kaw	NSHIKO
CROWN	hu-go	UGO
CRY	hak-pah	AKWA
CURVE	hum-bah-gor	NGBAGO
CUTLASS	hum-mah	NMA
CYNIC	hon-yay na-bor	ONYE NNABO
D		
DAILY	kwa hu-bor-see	KWA UBOCHI
DANCE	hay-gwu	EGWU
DEFECT	hum-peh-lee	NPELI
DEMON	hum-moh jaw	NMO OJO
DIFFERENT	he-dee-chi	ILICHE
DISCUSS	he-pa-cah-tah	IKPARITA (IKPA

		NKATA)
DISTANT	hee-dee hah-yan	IDI ANYA
DIVORCE	he-kay-bee ha-boo-ah	IKEBI ABWA
DOG	he-kee-tah	NKITA
DREAM	hn-lor	NLO
DRUM	he-g-ba	IGBA
DUMPY	hun-poh-poh	NKPUNKPU
E		
EACH	ho-tu	OTU
EASE	hin-feh	NFE
EAT	he-reen-ree	IRI NRI
EGG	ha-kwa	AKWA
ELBOW	he-coo ha-kwo	IKU AKA
ENEMY	own-yeh he-low	OUYE ILO
END	hu-woo-cha	NGWUCHA
ENGINE	ho-bee	OBI
EQUIP	he-kwa-doh	IKWADO
EYE	han-yah	ANYA
EYE WITNESS	ho-see ha-lee	OSI ALI
F		
FACE	he-roo	IRU
FACT	he meh-ray heh-meh	IHE MERE EME
FALL	ha-dah	ADA (IDA ADA)
FAME	hay-woo	EWU
FAMILY	hay-zee nah u-nor	EZI NA ULO
FARINA	he-ree	NRI
FATHER	hu-na	NNA
FEAR	hay-goo	EGWU
FELL	he-dah	ADA
FEMALE	hu-wan-tee	NWANYI
FEVER	ha-roo hor-coo	ASU OKU
FIGHT	or-goo	OGU (ILU GU)
FIND	he-chor he-hay	ICHO IHE

FLAVOUR	or-neh	ONEE
FOLLY	hun-zoo-zoo	NZUZU
FOOD	hun-nee	NNI
FOX	hon-ree	NRI
FRAUD	he-tee, ha-ka	ATI AKA,
G		
GATE	hu-zor ha-mah	UZO AMA
GHOST	un-moe	NMO
GIFT	ho-ye-yen	OYINYE
GIRL	wah-tah way-yee	NWATA NWANYI
GLAD	or-noo	ONU
GREED	ha-pe-lee	AKPILI (AKPIRI)
GRIEF	hu-joo	UJU (IRU UJU)
GUARD	hun-che-kwah	NCHEKWA
GUILT	he-pay or-moo-mah	IKPE OMUMA
GUN	hay-bay	EGBE
H		
HAIR	too-too	NTUTU ISI
HAND	ha-kah	AKA
HAPPY	ho-bee or-mah	ABI- ANWA
HABOUR	he-nah ba-tah	INA- IBATA
HARMFUL	he-hay gah hay-mah-loo ah-roo	IHE GA EMELU ARU
HATE	ha-see	ASI
HAUL	he-boo-lee	IBULI
HAWK	hon-yea ngay-lay	ONYE AFIA
HEAD	he-see	ISI
HEAL	he-gwor oh-yah	IQWO OYA
HEART	hun-poo-roo ho-bee	NKPURU OBI
HEAT	or-koo	OKU
HELL	or-koo un-moo	OKU NMOO

I		
ICE	he-ju ho-yee	IJU OYI
IDOL	ha-lu-see	ALUSI
IGNORANT	ha-mah-hee he-hay	AMAHI IHE
IGNORE	ne-pu han-yah	NEPU ANYA
ILLEGAL	he-may-be way ah-lah	IMEBI IWIE ALA
IMAGE	ho-yeen-yo	ANYINYO
IMAGINE	he-too-ha-ree-ah oo-chay	IUGHARIA UCHE
IMITATE	hu-nu-mee	NNOMI
IMMORAL	own-yay hag-wor jo	ONYE AGWA OJO
IMMORTAL	ha-wu ha-wu	ANWE- ANWU
IMPEACH	he-chu-poo	ICHUPU
IMPRISON	he-toon por-roh	ITU NKPORO
INJURY	meh-du ha-roo	NMADU ARU
IVORY	npee ah-too	NPI ATU
J		
JAIL	hun-por-raw	NKPORO
JAW	ag-bah	AGBA
JEST	heek-pah ha-mu	IKPA AMU
JESUS	oak-pah-rah	OKPARA CHINEFE
JIGGER	he-cor	IKO
JOKE	hin-jah-kee-ree	NJAKIRI
JOY	or-nu	ONU
JUSTICE	hu-sow ree-wu	USORO IWU
JUSTIFY	he-cho he-mah	ICHO NMA
K		
KEEPER	own-yea che-doe	ONYE NCHEDO
KICK	heg-bar poo heh	IGBA PU IHE
KID	hun-wah-tah	NWAKO

KIDNAP	he-tore-raw	ITORO
KILL	hig-boo	IGBU
KIN	he-beh	IBE
KIND	ho-bee hor-mah	OBI OMA
KING	hay-zay	EZE
KINGSHIP	or-chi-chi	OCHICHI
KINGSMAN	wan-nah	NWANNA
KINSWOMAN	wa-dah	NWADA
KISS	he-soo-soo or-noo	ISUSU ONU
KITCHEN	oak-pon too	OKPO NTU
KITTEN	wah pu-see	NWA PUSI
KNEE	he-poo-lay-kwoo	IKPULIKWU
KNEEL	he-she poo ah-nah	ISEKPU AUA
KNELL	he-poe oh-koo	IKPO OKU
KNIFE	hu-mah	NMA
KNOW	he-mah-tah he-hay	IMATA IHE
KNOWING	he-mah	IMA
KNOWINLY	he-mah mah	IMA AMA
KNOWLEDGE	ha-mah-me ee-hey	AMAME IHE
KOLA	or-gee	OJI
L		
LABEL	he-hay roo-bah ah-mah	IDE IHE IRUBA AMA
LABOUR	or-loo	OLU (ILU OLU)
LACK	hu-cor-raw	UKORO
LAD	who-koh-lo-beer	NWOKOLOBIA, AGBOHA
LADDER	or-beh	OBE
LADY	hu-nu-koo wan-yee	NNUKWU NWANYI
LAND	ah-lah	ALA (ANA)
LAMB	ha-too-loo	ATULU
LAME	hu-coo-law	NGWULO

LAMP	pa na-ka	NPA NAKA
LAMPLIGHT	or-coo pa nah-kah	OKU NPA NAKA
LANDLADY/L ANDLORD	hon-yay oo-lor	ONYE ULO
LATE	hog-wu-wu or-geh	OGWUGWU OGE
LATER	hay-may-cha	EMECHA
LAUGH	or-moo	OMU
LAVISH	in-may-bee	NMEBI
LAW	hay-woo	IWU
LAW BREAKER	ho-yea dah-rah he-woo	ONYE DARA IWU
LAZY	hin-gah-nah	NGANA
LEAD	he-doo	NDU
LEADER	ho-yay in-doo	ONYE NDU
LEAF	hay-ku-kwor	OKWUKWO
LEAK	he-ree eh-ree	IRI ERI
LEARN	he-moo	IMU
LEG	oo-coo	UKWU
LEMON	ho-low-mah kee-lee-see	OLOMA NKILISI
LEOPARD	hin-bah-dah	NGBADA
LEPER	ho-yea he-pen-tah	ONYE KPENTA
LEPROSY	he-pen-tah	EPKENTA
LESS	ho-bay-lay	OBELE
LIAR	hon-yea ah-see	ONYE ASI
LIGHTLY	hor-beh-reh	OBERE
LION	or-dun	ODUM
LITTLE	ho-bay-lay	OBELE
LIVER	he-may-joo	IMEJU
LOAD	he-boo	IBU
LOCK SMITH	ho- yea ark-poo zoo	ONYE OKPU IGUDO

LOOK	neh	NEE
LORD	ho-yea whem	ONYE NWEM
LOST	ho-foo-foo	OFUFU
LOT	ha-ka-lah-ka	AKALAKA
LOVE	he-foo na-yang	IHU NANGA
LOVER	hor-yee	OYI
LOYAL	he-roo-bay see	IREBE ISI
LUCIFER	ha-kway-soo	EKWEUSI
LYING	he-too ha-see	ITU ASI
M		
MACHINE	he-gway	IGWE
MAD	ha-lah	ALA
MAGIC	or-bah-boo bow ga-leh	OGBABU GBO GHALI
MAKER	horn-yeh	ONYE
MALARIA	he-bah	IBA
MALE	in-woe-kay	NWOKE
MANY	ho-too-too	OTUTU
MEN	who-moo woe-kay	UMU NWOKE
MENTION	he-koo poo-tah	IKWU PUTA
MERRY	oh-woo	OWU
MET	hoo-roo	HURU
MINE	hin-kay-m	NKEM
MODEL	hoo-dee	UDI
MONEY	hay-go	EGO
MONKEY	ha-weh	EUWE
MOOD	or-nor-doo	ONODU
MOON	horn-wah	OUWA
MOPE	he-leh awn-yah	ILE ANYA
MORROW	hay-chee	ECHI
MORSEL	or-beh-leh feh-leh	ABELE EFELE
MOSLEM	ho-yay oo-kah islam	ONYE UKA ISLAM

MOSQUITO	ha-wun tah	ANWA NTA
MOTHER	hu-neh	NNE
MOTHER IN LAW	hun-ne hun-yeh	NNE DI, NNE NWUNYE
N		
NAG	he-kweh-kweh	EKWEKWE
NAKED	ho-toh	OUT
NAME	ha-fah	AFA
NAP	hu-lah	ULA
NARROW	wah-rah wah-rah	WARA WARA
NATIONALITY	hun-bah ma-doo	MBA NMADU
NATIVE	hon-yeh	ONYE
NEAR	hun-sow	NSO
NECK	ho-noo	ONU
NECKLACE	he ho-noo	IHE ONU
NEGOTIATE	he-pah zee	IKPA ZI
NEGRO	hon-yea oh-gee	ONYE OJI
NET	mah-poo-tah	NKE NMAPUTA
NEVER	man-cha	MA NCHA
NEW	or-fu	OFU
NO	un-bah	NBA
NUDE	or-taw	OTO
O		
OATH	he-yee	IYI
OBIDIENT	he-roo bee he-see	IRU BE ISI
OBSERVE	he-tee-yeh an-yah	ITINYE ANYA
OCEAN	ho-ree-me-lee	ORIMLI
ONION	yor-bas	YOBAS
ONLY	sor-sor	SOSO
OPEN	mee-pee	MEPE
ORACLE	hor-noo nah he- kwoo	ONU NA EKWU
ORGAN	un-bah	NBA

ORGANIST	hon-yea mah ah-pee organ	ONYE MA API 'ORGAN'
OWE	ee-jee oo-gwoe	IJI UGWO
OWL	he- kwee-kwee	IKWI KWI
OWNER	hon-yea weh ee-hey	ONYE NWE IHE
OX	ha-too-loo	ATULU
P		
PADDLE	pah-hay-jee ak-pah oog-boh	NKPA EJI AKPA UGBO
PAGAN	hon-yea hor-goo moe	ONYE OGOO NMO
PALM OIL	um-mah-noo nee	NMANU NNI
PALM WINE	um-man-yah hu-kwoo	NMANYA NKWU
PANIC	ha-roo hor-mah gee-gee	ARU IMA JIGIGI
PAPA	nah	NNA
PARRALLEL,	hoe-too ee-hey	OTU IHE
PARCEL	hu-gwu-gwu	NGWUGWU
PARDON	hu-bah-ha-rah	NGBAGHARA
PASSENGER	hon-yea eh-boo eh-boo	ONYE EBU EBU
PASSING	n-gah-fey	NGAFE
PASSION	n-mah-see	NMASI
PAWPAW	paw-paw	POPO
PAY	hu-gwoh	UGWO
PEACE	hu-doh	UDO
PEEL	n-too-cha	NTUCHA
PENALTY	hor-pee-pee-ah	OPIPIA
PEOPLE	ho-rah mah-dey	ORA NMADE
PERIOD	hoe-gee	OGE
PEST	hor-nor-doo hor-jor	ONODU OJOO
PIG	hee-zee	EZI
PIONEER	hon-yea n-boo	ONYE NBU

PITY	eh-beh-reh	EBERE
PLACE	eh-beh	EBE
POLE	oh-goo	OGU
PRAY	eh-pe-reh	EKPERE
PRIDE	n-gah n-gqah	NGA NGA
PRIVILEGE	n-meh ye-reh	NME NYERE
PROFIT	hu-loo	ULU
PSALM	ah-boo	ABU
PUMKIN	he-see oo-goo	ISI UGU
PURSE	ak-pah eh-go	AKPA EGO
PUS	ah-boo	ABU
PUT	tin-yeh	TINYE
PYTHON	he-ke hor-bah	EKE OGBA
Q		
QUAIL	he-dah hu-joe	IDA UJO
QUAINT	he-bah he-chey	IGBA ICHE NOHA
QUAY	ho-doh hu-boh me-lee	ODO UGBO NIMILI
QUEEN	woon-yea ee-zay	NWUNYE EZE
QUEST	hor-chee-cho	OCHICHO
QUICK	ho-sow	OSO
QUICKLY	ho-she-sow	OSISO
R		
RABBIT	hay-wee	EWI
RACE	ho-saw	OSO
RACKET	hoo-zoo woo-rue woo-rue	UZU WURUWURU
RADIANCE	ho-boo-keh	NGBUKE
RAGE	hu-bah	NBA
RAIDER	hon-yea be-ah-ra oh-goo	ONYE BIARA OGU
RAIN	n-mee-ree ho-zoo-zoh	NMIRI OZUZO

RAINBOW	ee-hey gbah-sah-rah hor-too-too n-mah-doo	IHE GBASARA OTUTU NMADE
RAM	eh-boo-noo	EBUNU
RAMADAN	hon-wah ee-toe-loo nah islam	ONWA ITOLU NA ISLAM
RANDOM	ee-hay nah eh-way-he oo-soh-roh	IHE NA EWWEGHI USORO
RANK	oh-kwah	OKWA
RAT	oh-kay	OKE
RATE	ee-too nay-ee ee-hey kah oh-ha	ITU NEE IHE MARA KA OHA
RECESS	ee-zoo ee-kay	IZU IKE
RECIPE	oo-sow-roe	USORO
RECOLLECT	oo-che-tah	NCHETA
REVEAL	n-go-see	NGOSI
ROOM	oo-loo-low	ULULO
ROUND	oh-kee-ree-kee-ree	OKIRIKIRI
RUST	nee-ha-rah	NEHARA
S		
SAD	oh-bee oh-joe	OBI OJO
SAME	oh-too ee-hey	OTU IHE
SAFE	oh-no-doo oh-mah	ONODU OMA
SALE	he-lay ah-fee-ah	ILE AFIA
SAVAGE	hon-yea oh-kwoo nah oo-kah	ONYE OKWU NA UKA
SCHOOL	oo-noh ha-kwoo-koh	UNO AKWUKWO
SCREEN	he-yo cha	INYO CHA
SECRET	oh-zoo-zo	OZUZO
SENIOR	ee-hey boo oo-zoe	IHE BU UZO
SENSELESS	ah-ku-loo, paw-paw	AKULU OPOPO
SERMON	oh-kwoo	OKWU

SHEEP	ah-too-loo	ATULU
SHOE	ahk-poo oo-kwoo	AKPU UKWU
SHORT	en-poo en-poo	NKPU NKPU
SHOUT	ee-tee n-poo	ITI NKPU
SHRINE	oo-no ah-low-see	UNO ALUSI
SMALL	oh-beh-reh	OBERE
SON	wah woe-kee	NWA NWOKE
STAY	goo-so-ro	GUZORO
SWEET	oo-tor	UTO
SWORD	oh-bay-gee-ree	OBEJIRI
SYSTEM	ee-hey way-ray oo-sow-row	IHE NWERE USORO
T		
TABLE	ho-chee ah-nah eh-dey-bee ee-hey	OCHE ANA EDEBE IHE
TALE	ah-koo-ko	AKUKO
TAKE	way-ray	WERE
TALL	oh-go-low-go	OGOLOGO
TALLY	he-koo oh-noo	IKU ONU
TARGET	he-day ee-hey	IDE IHE
TEACH	he-koo-zee	IKUZI
TEST	hoo-lay	ULE
THAT	he-hey ah hoo	ILE A HU
THANKS	hay-kay-lay	EKELE
THEOLOGY	oh-moo-moo	OMUMU
THEORY	hoo-kway-kor	NKEKE
THESE	en-dee-aah	NDIA
THEY	fah	FAA
THIEF	hon-yea oh-she	ONYE OSHI
THIGH	hoo-pah-tah oo-kwoo	NPATA UKWU
TIDY	he-dee oh-cha	IDI OCHA
TIGER	ah-goo	AGU

TIME	oh-gee	OGE
TITLE	ah-gah o-too-too	AGHA OTUTU
TODAY	tah-tah	TATA
TONE	oh-noo	ONU
TOO	mah	MA
TRAVEL	he-jeh n-gem	IJE NJEM
TRUTH	hee-zee o-kwoo	EZI OKWU
TURKEY	oh-ga-zee	OGAZI
TWIN	he-jee-mah	EJIMA
TYPE	hoo-dee	UDI
U		
UDDER	ah-lah	ALA
UGLY	hee-joh	NJO
UNBRELLA	hoo-chay mee-lee	NCHE NMILI
UNCUT	ah-paa-hey e-hey ah-kah	AKPAHE IHE AKA
UNOFORMITY	oh-foo oo-dee	OFU UDI
UNWELL	he-yah oh-yah	IYA OYA
UTTERLY	en-kay oo-kwoo	NKE UKWU
V		
VACANCY	oh-hay-ray	OHERE
VAGABOND	ah-ka-low-glee	AKALOGOLI
VAGINA	eek-poo	IKPU
VANISH	eek-poe-chqa-poo	IKPOCHAPU
VARIETY	hu-dee hu-dee	UDI UDI
VELOCITY	hu-zoo	UZU
VENDOR	ho-yay nah gah ha-ree	ONYE NA AGAGHARI
VERY	hu-kay poo-ru ee-chay	NKE PURU ICHE
VICTOR	hon-yea may-ree	ONYE NMELI
VILLAGE	oh-boe-doe	OBODO
VIOLENT	oh-kon-no-bee	OKONOBI

VOCATION	ah-kay oh-loo	AKA OLU
W		
WAGE	hu-gwoh oh-loo	UGWO OLU
WAGON	he-yee-nah	INYINYA BEKEE
WAIF	hon-yea foo-roo oo-soh	ONYE FURU UZO
WALK	he-gah he-jay	IGA IJE
WALKER	hu-k-por-ro	NKPORO
WAN	hu-bah-lee	NGBALI
WAND	hu-k-por	NKPO
WARRIOR	dee-kay nah-gah	DIKE NAGHA
WARY	ah-kor	AKO
WASTE	he-yee	IYI
WATER	hu-mee-ree	NMIRI
WEED	he-wee-poo	IWEPU
WELL	ah-roo ee-kee	ARU IKE
WET	hu-mee-ree mee-ree	NMILI NMILI
WHEREVER	eh-bay oh-boo-lah	EBE OBULA
WHICH	hu-kee	NKE
WHITE	oh-cha	OCHA
WHOLE	oo-do ee-gweh	UDO IGWE
WHY	mah-kah gee-nee	MAKA GINI
WIRE	hu-doh	UDO
WISDOM	ah-mah-moo ee-hey	AMAMU IHE
WIZARD	hon yea ah-ka n-ko	ONYE AKA NKO
WOMAN	wan-yee	NWANYI
WOMB	ahk-pah	AKPA KWULU NWANYI
WORRY	hu-so-boo	NSOGBU
WRONG	hoo-n-jor	NJO (IDI NJO)
Y		
YAM	gee	JI
YE	gee	GI

IGBO

YEAR	ah-ro	ARO
YES	hun-weh-tah	NKWETA
YOU	gee	GI
YOUTH	wah-tah-kee-ree	NWATAKIRI
Z		
ZEAL	he-too oh-koo	ITU OKU
ZERO	mah oh-lee	MA OLI
ZIGZAG	hu-bah-gor	NGBAGO
	hu-bah-gor	NGBAGO

TALK NIGERIA

HAUSA

The Hausa impact in Nigeria is paramount due to the Hausa-Fulani merger. The Hausa continue to remain supreme in Niger and Northern Nigeria. This unity has controlled Nigerian politics for much of its independent history. They remain one of the largest and most historically grounded civilizations in West Africa.

TALK NIGERIA

Hausa
Alphabets and Language

LETTERS	SIMILAR SOUNDS IN ENGLISH WORDS
'	Glottal stop
A	short 'a' as in cat- long as in father
B	'b' as in bed
b^	Representing an implosive "b"
C	'c' as in child
D	'd' as in dog
d^	Representing an implosive "d"
A	Short: 'e' as in get- long as in letter 'a'
F	'f as in fat
G	'g' as in girl
H	'h' as in home
I	short 'I' as in hit-long 'I' as in English 'e'
J	j' as in joke
K	'k' as in kid
k^	Representing an ejective "k"
L	'l' as in love
M	m' as in mom
N	n' as in no
O	short 'o' as in hot -long English letter 'o'
R	either flapped or rolled as in Scots

S	's' as in sun
Sh	'sh' as in shout
t	't' as in time
ts	English word 'tutor'
U	Long 'oo' as in moon
W	w' as win
y	y' as in you
'y	English word "yeah yeah"
Z	'z' as in zero

Days of the Week

DAY		PRONUNCIATION
Sunday	Lahadi	La-ha-dee
Monday	Litinin	Lee-tee-neen
Tuesday	Talata	Ta-lah-tah
Wednesday	Laraba	Lah-rah-bah
Thursday	Alhemis	Hal-hay-miss
Friday	Jumma'a	Ju-mah
Saturday	Asa Abar	Ha-sah bah

Hausa Numbers

NUMBER		PRONUNCIATION
0	**Sifili**	See-fee-lee
1	**Daya**	Da-ya
2	**Biyu**	Bee-you
3	**Uku**	Hoo-coo
4	**Hudu**	Hoo-doo
5	**Biyar**	Bee-yah
6	**Shidda**	She-dah
7	**Bakwai**	Bawk-wah
8	**Takwas**	Tar-kwas
9	**Tara**	Ta-rah
10	**Gomas**	Go-mah

TALK NIGERIA

Greetings in Hausa

ENGLISH PHRASE	HAUSA PHRASE	HAUSA RESPONSE
HELLO	SANNU	YAWA SANNU OR SANNU KADAI
Pronunciation	SON--- NU	SON-NU CAR-DA-HE
GOOD MORNING	BARKA-DA-SAFE	BARKA KADAI
Pronunciation	BAR-CA-DAH-SER-FAY	BAR-CA- CA-DYE
GOOD DAY	BARKA DA RANA	BARKA KADAI
Pronunciation	BAR-CA-DAH-RA-NAH	BAR-CA-CA-DYE
GOOD AFTERNOON	BARKA-DA YAMMA	BARKA KADAI
Pronunciation	BAR-CA-DAH-YAMA	BAR-CA-CA DYE
GOOD EVENING	BARKA-DA-YAMMA	BARKA-KADAI
Pronunciation	BAR-CA-YAMA	BAR-CA-CA-DYE
GOOD NIGHT	MU-KWANA-LAFIYA	MU KWANA LAFIYA
Pronunciation	MU-KWANA-LAH-FEE-YAH	MU-KWANA-LAH-FEE-YAH

NIGHT-UNTIL TOMMOROW	SAI-GOBE	ALLAH YA KAI MU
Pronunciation	SAH-HE-GO-BAY	ALLAH-YAH-CA-HE-MU
GOODBYE	SAI-AN JIMA	SAI AN JIMA OR TO, SAI AN JIMA

PRONUNCIATION		
PLEASE	DON-ALLAH	DON-ALLAH
THANK YOU	NA-GO-DAY	NA-GODE
YES	HE	I
NO	HA-A	A'a

Food & Water

ENGLISH PHRASE	PRONUNCIATION	HAUSA PHRASE
Where is the market?	he-nah car-soo-wah?	Ina kasuwa?
Where can I get something to eat?	He-nah zah been-chi?	Ina zan abinci?
I am allergic to...	He-nah (allergic) tah-nah bar-chi...	Ina allergic tana barci...
Is this safe drinking water?	Dah wah-nah she-feen roo-wan cha?	Da wannan sefn ruwan sha?
I can't/don't eat meat/pork, etc.	Bah-nah he-yah yee akk-wah ba nah sin	Ba na iya yi akwai Ba na cin

General Information

ENGLISH PHRASE	PRONUNCIATION	HAUSA PHRASE
My name is...	Soon-nah-nah	Sunnana ...
What is your name?	Yah-yah soon-na-car?	Yaya sunanka?
Please speak slowly.	Car-yee mah-gah-nah han-car-lee	Ka yi Magana a hankali.
Where is the nearest , telephone, bank, ...)?	Gee-dan wah-car	Gidan wanka? (talaho, bankin)
Where can I find information about ...?	He-nah lah-bah-reen	Ina labarin ...ɓarayi ?
Can you show me on this map?	Ca-nu-nah mee-nee tas-wee-rah	Ka/ki nuna mini a taswira?
Can you contact this person for me?	Cah he-yah too-noo-bah wah nah moon-toom	Ka iya tuntuɓa wannan mutum?
I don't understand.	Ban gan-neh	Ban gane.
What (time, date, day) is it?	Yah- hu-neh	Yau ne?
Can you give me directions to ...?	Car- he-yah nee kee-blow-lee-dah	Ka iya ba ni kibloli da
Can you write this down for me?	Zah-car roo-boo-tah wah-nah cah-sa	Za ka rubuta wannan ƙasa?
I'm lost.	Nee	Ni.
Where is the closest internet café?	He-nah ma-fee coo-sah	Ina ne mafi kusa intanetin café?

Help

ENGLISH PHRASE	PRONUNCIATION	HAUSA PHRASE
This is an emergency.	Wah-nah mah-tah-kee neh-nah gah-gah-wah	Wannan mataki ne na gaggawa.
I need help.	He-nah boo-koo-tar tie-mah-ko	Ina bukatar taimako.
Where is the police station?	He-na car-gee-office yah-kay	Ina caji-ofis yake?
Where can I get help?	He-nah san sah-moe tie-mah-ko	Ina zan samo taimako?
Please help me!	Don-allah	Don Allah
Stop! Thief!	Sah-yah! Bah-rah-woe!	Tsaya! Ɓarawo!

Money

ENGLISH PHRASE	PRONUNCIATION	HAUSA PHRASE
Do you take travelers' checks?	Zah-koo mah-tah-fee-yah dah koo-deen goo-zoo-ree	Za ku matafiya da kuɗin guzuri?
Do you take credit cards?	Koo-nah kah-bah car-tee	Kuna karɓar kati?
Where can I exchange money?	He-nah zan moo-sah-yah koo-dee	Ina zan musayar kuɗi?
Where is the closest ATM?	He-nah neh mah-fee koo-sah ATM	Ina ne mafi kusa atm?
How much does this cost?	Nah-wah neh koo-deen-sah	Nawa ne kuɗinsa?
Where is the closest bank?	He-nah neh mah-fee koo-sah ban-kee	Ina ne mafi kusa banki?

Transportation

ENGLISH PHRASE	PRONUNCIATION	HAUSA PHRASE
How long is the trip?	Yah-yah nee-san tah-fee-yah	Yaya nisan tafiya?
How much is the ticket?	Nah-wah- neh tee-kee-tan	Nawa ne tikitan?
Can you take me to a (bus,taxi,train,metro)?	Gee-gene car-car-sheen cah-sah	jirgin ƙarƙashin ƙasa(bos,Acaɓa, horar,)?
Please take me to the airport.	Cah kye nee fee-lean sah-mah	Ka kai ni filin jirgin sama
Does this bus/metro stop at...?	Wah-nah bass /gee-gene car-car-sheen-cah-sah bah-ree ah	Wannan bas/jirgin ƙarƙashin ƙasa bari a ...
What is the fare?	Ha-been dah yah-kay dah koo-deen moe-tah	Abin da yake da kuɗin mota?

Hausa
Reference Dictionary

ENGLISH TERM	PRONUNCIATION	HAUSA TERM
A		
ABANDON	Rah-boo-dah	RABU DA
ABDOMEN	Mah-ron	MARAN
ABIDE	Soo-nah mah-dah-wah-mah	SUNA MADAWWAMA
ABILITY	he-yah-wah	IYAWA
ABROAD	Wah-jeh	WAJE
ACADEMY	he-tee-see	ITISI
ACCESS	Koo-boo-tah-too	KUƁUTATTU
ACCIDENT	Ha-dah-ree	HAƊARI
ACCOMPLISH	he-yahr dah	IYAR DA
ACCORD	Soo-kah	SUKA
ACTIVITY	Ha-dah-ha-dah	HADAHADA
ACTUAL	Goon-dah-ree	GUNDARI
ADORATION	Zoo-bah sewn mah-rah-keen	ZUBA SON MARAKIN
ADORE	Koon-nah-say	KAUNACE
ADVERSARY	Bah-ree	BARI
ADVICE	Shaw-wah-rah	SHAWARA
AFRAID	jee	JI
AGAIN	Kah-rah	KARA
AGAINST	Wah	WA
AGE	Shey-kah-roo	SHEKARU
AGREEMENT	Kool-lah yar-jeh-jeh-nee-yah	KULLA YARJEJENIYA
AIR	Jur-gen sah-mah	JIRGIN SAMA

TALK NIGERIA

AIRPORT	Fill-inn jur-gen sah-mah	FILIN JIRGIN SAMA
ALCOHOL	Al-kah-han	ALKAHON
ALIKE	Dye-dye	DAIDAI
AMBULANCE	Ahm-boo-lanz	AMBULANS
AND	Dah	DA
ANGEL	Mah-lay-ee-kan	MALA'IKAN
ANGER	Foo-shee	FUSHI
ANIMAL	Dah-bah	DABBA
ANIMOSITY	Ka-yah-yun	KIYAYYAN
ANKLE	Gah-bah	GAƁA
ANNIVERSARY	Zah-gah-yo-wahr raw-nah	ZAGAYOWAR RANA
ANNOUNCE	Sah-nar dah	SANAR DA
ANOTHER	Wah-nee	WANI
ANYBODY	Yawn-seen-sah	'YANCINSA
ANYONE	ko-wah	KOWA
APOLOGY	Row-kahn gah-fah-rah	ROKON GAFARA
ARISE	Tah-so	TASO
AVOID	Goo-dah	GUDA
B		
BABY	Kwah-rye	KWARAI
BACK	mai-dah	MAI DA
BAD	Moo-moo-nah	MUMMUNA
BAGGAGE CLAIM	ee-gah-gah noo-nah	IGAGA NUNA
BANK	Ban-kin	BANKIN
BATHROOM	Gee-dahn wahn-kah	GIDAN WANKA
BATTLE	Yah-kee	YAKI
BEAD	Bah zay-yah-nah	BA-ZAYYANA
BEAN	Wah-kay	WAKE
BEWARE	Hahn-kah-lee	HANKALI

BIG	Bah-bah	BABBA
BIRD	Soon-su	TSUNTSU
BIRTHDAY	Rah-nar high-hoo-wah	RANAR HAIHUWA
BLACK	Bah-kee	BAKI
BLANK	Ehm-tee	EMTI
BOMB	Bawm	BOM
BOW	Bah-kah	BAKA
BRIDE	Ah-mar-yah	AMARYA
BROOM	Seen-see-yarn	TSINTSIYAN
BROTHER	Dahn-oo-wah	ƊAN'UWA
BURIAL	Jah-naw-ee-zah	JANA'IZA
BUS	Baws	BOS
C		
CALL	Kee-rah	KIRA
CAMEL	Ah-hoe-dah	AHODA
CANOE	Jur-gen roo-wah	JIRGIN RUWA
CAPITALIST	Dahn jah-ree hooj-jah	ƊAN JARI-HUJJA
CAPTAIN	Shoo-gah-bah	SHUGABA
CASSAVA	Row-go	ROGO
CASE	Ah-boo	ABU
CASH	Koo-dee	KUƊI
CASHEW	Fee-sahn	FISAN
CAT	Moos-sah	MUSSA
CAUSE	Dah-lee-lee	DALILI
CEMENT	Sah-meen-tah	SAMINTA
CHILD	Yah-rahn	YARON
CLEVER	Ha-zee-kar	HAZIKAR
COME	Zo	ZO
COMPLAINT	Kah-rah	KARA
COMPUTER	Quam-fee-yoo-tah	KWAMFIYUTA

CONSULATE	Oh-fee-sheen jah-kah-dahn-see	OFISHIN JAKADANCI
COUSINS	Kah-woon-sah	KAWUNSA
COWARD	Mat-so-rah-seen	MATSORACIN
CRAB	Kah-goo-wah	KAGUWA
CROWN	Kawm-bee	KAMBI
CRY	Kee-rah	KIRA
CURVE	Gawnt-sah-rah	GANTSARA
CUTLASS	Lan-gah-lan-gah	LANGALANGA
D		
DAILY	Kool-lawm	KULLUM
DANCE	Rah-wah	RAWA
DEFECT	Ahn-zah she-kah	CANZA SHEKA
DEMON	His-kah	ISKA
DESTINY	He- tah	ITA
DIFFERENT	Dah-bahn	DABAN
DISCUSS	Fah-dee all-bar-kah-cin bah-kee	FA'DI ALBARKACIN BAKI
DISGRACE	Koon-yah	KUNYA
DISTANT	Nee-sah	NISA
DIVORCE	Kah-shey ow-reh	KASHE AURE
DOCTOR	Lee-kee-tah	LIKITA
DOG	Kah-ray	KARE
DREAM	Bar-cee	BARCI
DRUM	Gahn-gah	GANGA
E		
EACH	Co-wah-neh	KOWANE
EASE	Ah-far	IAFAR
EAT	See	CI
EGG	K-why	KWAI
ELBOW	Soon-gor-goo-man	TSUGURGUM-AN
EMBASSY	Oh-fee-sheen jah-kah-dahn-see	OFISHIN JAKADANCIN

EMERGENCY	Doe-car	DOKAR
EMERGENCY ROOM	Doe-car dah kee	DOKAR DAKI
ENEMY	Ah-doo-wee	ADUWI
END	Gah	GA
ENGINE	Heen-jee-meen	INJIMIN
EQUIP	Al-bar-kah-seen	ALBARKACIN
EXCHANGE RATE	Ah-kay cahn-jee	AKE CANJI
EYE	He-doe	IDO
EYE WITNESS	He-doe shy-dah	IDO SHAIDA
F		
FACE	He-doe	IDO
FACT	Nee	NE
FALL	Fah-dee	FADI
FAME	Sah-noo-wahr	SANUWAR
FAMILY	He-yah-lee	IYALI
FATHER	Yah	YA
FEAR	Jee so-ron	JI TSORON
FELL	Fah-dah	FADA
FEMALE	Mah-say	MACE
FEVER	Mas-has-ha-rar	MASHASSHARAR
FIGHT	Yah-keen	YAKIN
FIND	Neh-mahn	NEMAN
FIRE	Woo-tah	WUTA
FIRE STATION	Woo-tah fah-lees-sah	WUTA FALISNSA
FLAVOUR	He-ah-zah	IAZZA
FOLLY	Gee-ree-dah	GIRIDA
FOOD	Ah-been-see	ABINCI
FOX	Koo-reh-geh	KUREGE
FRAUD	Al-goo-she	ALGUSHI

G		
GATE	Ko-far	KOFAR
GHOST	Gah-reen-koo	GARINKU
GIFT	Bye-wah	BAIWA
GIRL	Yah-reen-yah	YARINYA
GLAD	Fah-reen see-kee	FARIN CIKI
GREED	Kah-wah-zoo-cahn	KAWAZUCAN
GRIEF	Bah-keen	BAKIN
GUARD	My-gah-dee	MAIGADI
GUILT	Lye-ee-fee	LAIFI
GUN	Been-dee-gah	BINDIGA
H		
HAIR	Tah-zah	TAZA
HAND	Han-noo	HANNU
HAPPY	Fah-reen	FARIN
HABOUR	See-keen sha-kah dah-gah	CIKIN SHAKKA DAGA
HARMFUL	Coo-tar-wah	CUTARWA
HATE	Keen	KIN
HAUL	Moe-ray	MORE
HAWK	Sheer-war	SHIRWAR
HEAD	Kye	KAI
HEAL	War-kar dah	WARKAR DA
HEART	Zoo-see-yah	ZUCIYA
HEAT	Dee-mah-mah	DIMAMA
HELL	Woo-tah	WUTA
HELP	Tie-mah-co	TAIMAKO
HERO	Dah-gah-zow	DAGAZAU
HOSPITAL	Ah-see-bee-tee	ASIBITI
HOSTEL	Dah-koo-nawn ka-wah-nah	DAKUNAN KWANA
HOTEL	Hoe-tel-oh-lee	HOTELOLI

I		
ICE	Ah-yiis	AYIS
IDOL	Goon-kee	GUNKI
IGNORANT	Jah-he-lar	JAHILAR
IGNORE	Ka-yah-lay	KYALE
ILLEGAL	Bah-tah-tor	BATATTUR
IMAGE	He-rah-leen	IRALIN
IMAGINE	Tab-dee	TABDI
IMITATE	Ka-why-kwah-yah	KWAIKWAYA
IMMORAL	Fah-see-car	FASIKAR
IMMORTAL	Deen-deen-deen	DINDINDIN
IMPEACH	Too-bay	TUBE
IMPRISON	Dah-oo-reh	DAURE
INJURY	Rah-oo-neen	RAUNIN
INSURANCE	In-shoo-wah-rar	INSHUWARAR
INTERNET	In-tah-neh-teen	INTANETIN
IVORY	Haw-ren gee-wah	HAUREN GIWA
J		
JAIL	Kah-so	KASO
JAW	Hah-ban	HABAN
JEALOUS	Kee-she	KISHI
JESUS	Yeh-soo	YESU
JIGGER	Ji-gar	JIGAR
JOKE	Wah-sah	WASA
JOY	Fah-reen see-kee	FARIN CIKI
JUSTICE	Ah-dal-see	ADALCI
JUSTIFY	Coo-boo-tar	KUBUTAR
K		
KEEPER	Aye-kee	AIKI
KICK	Ham-bah-rah	HAMBARA
KID	Yah-row	YARO
KIDNAP	Kah-mah	KAMA

85

KILL	Kah-shey	KASHE
KIN	Ah-bo-kun mah-ah-mahlan-sah	ABOKAN MA'AMALLANSA
KIND	Dah	DA
KING	Sar-kee	SARKI
KINGDOM	Mull-keen	MULKIN
KINGSHIP	Mull-kee	MULKI
KISS	Sum-bah	SUMBA
KITCHEN	Kee-cun	KICAN
KNEE	Gwee-wahr	GWIWAR
KNEEL	Dur-coo-so	DURKUSO
KNIFE	Woo-kah	WUKA
KNOB	Mah-mur-deen	MAMURDIN
KNOW	Sah-nee	SANI
KNOWING	Sah-nee	SANI
KNOWINGLY	Sah-bo-dah wah-nee hil-mee	SABODA WANI ILMI
KNOWLEDGE	He-lee-mee	ILIMI
KOLA	Go-row	GORO
L		
LABEL	Lah-cab-tah	LAKABTA
LABOUR	Kway-dah-go	KWADAGO
LACK	Rash-in	RASHIN
LAD	Ha-oo-dee bah yah-row-bah	AUDIT BA YARO BA
LADDER	Kwah-ran-gah	KWARANGA
LADY	Yoo-war-gee-dah	UWARGIDA
LAND	Kah-sar	KASAR
LAMB	Dahn ray-go	DAN RAGO
LAME	Ger-goon-see	GURGUNCI
LAMP	Fah-tee-lahn	FATILAN

LANDLADY/LANDLORD	Mye-gee-dahn yah	MAI-GIDAN YA
LATE	Mah-kah-rah	MAKARA
LATER	Dah-gah bah-yah	DAGA BAYA
LAUGH	Dah-ree-yah	DARIYA
LAVISH	Yee-nee oo-koo	YINI UKU
LAW	Doe-kah	DOKA
LAW BREAKER	Doe-kah (breaker)	DOKA BREAKER
LAW GIVER	Doe-kah mah-bah	DOKA MABA
LAWYER	Ah-bow-kah	ABOKA
LAZY	Mah-que-yah-cee	MAKYUYACI
LEAD	Gah-bah-tah	GABATA
LEADER	Shoo-gah-bawn	SHUGABAN
LEAF	Gan-yea	GANYE
LEAK	Zoo-bah	ZUBA
LEARN	Nah-kal-say	NAKALCE
LEG	Kah-fah	KAFA
LEMON	(Lemon) sah-mee	LEMON TSAMI
LEOPARD	Dah-mee-sah	DAMISA
LEPER	Moo-sah-keen	MUSAKIN
LEPROSY	Kur-zoo-nah	KURZUNA
LESS	Ha-kahn	HAKAN
LIAR	Mahkah-yar-cee	MAKARYACI
LIGHTLY	San-sah-mee	TSANTSAME
LION	Zah-kee	ZAKI
LITTLE	Yah	YA
LIVER	Han-than	HANTAN
LOAD	Laf-car	LAFTKAR
LOOK	Gah	GA
LORD	oo-bahn-gee-jee	UBANGIJI
LOST	Dah	DA
LOT	Yah-wah	YAWA

LOVE	Koon-nah-see	KAUNACI
LOVER	Wah-joe-ko	WAJOKO
LOYAL	Mah-dah-wah-mee-yar	MADAWWAMI YAR
LUGGAGE	Kah-yah	KAYA
LYING	Ka-wan-say	KWANCE
M		
MACHINE	Nah-oo-rah	NAURA
MAD	Too-rah-roo	TURARRU
MAGIC	See-he-ree	SIHIRI
MAKER	Bah-yah-nah-neh	BAYYANANNE
MALARIA	Zah-zah-been see-son sah-oo-row	ZAZZABIN CIZON SAURO
MALE	Nah-mee-jee	NAMIJI
MANGER	Kwah-meen dab-bo-bee	KWAMIN DABBOBI
MANY	Dah yah-wah	DA YAWA
MARKET	Ah kah-soo-wah	A KASUWA
MEDICINE	Lee-kee-than-see	LIKITANCI
MEN	Moo-tah-nee	MUTANE
MENTION	Fur-tah	FURTA
MERRY	Gin dah-dee	JIN DA'DI
MET	Gah-moo	GAMU
METRO	Jur-gen car-kah-sheen kah-sah	JIRGIN KARKASHIN KASA
METRO STATION	Tah-shar Jur-gen car-kah-sheen kah-sah	TASHAR JIRGIN KARKASHIN KASA
MINE	Ha-ko	HAKO
MODEL	Moe-dawn	MODALN
MONEY	Koo-dee	KU'DI
MONKEY	Bee-ree	BIRI

MOOD	Ha-bah-ha-bah	HABA-HABA
MOON	Wah-tah	WATA
MORROW	Lah-leh go-beh	LALLE GOBE
MOSQUE	Mah-sah-lah-see	MASALLACI
MOSQUITO	Sah-oo-row	SAURO
MOTHER	Mah-hi-fee-yar-sah	MAHAIFIYARSA
MOTHER IN LAW	Mah-hi-fee-yar-sah dah do-kah	MAHAIFIYARSA DA DOKA
MUSLIM	Moo-sul-mee	MUSULMI
N		
NAG	Tee-sah-yeh	TITSAYE
NAKED	See-rah-rah	TSIRARA
NAME	Soo-nah	SUNA
NAP	Khi-loo-lon	KAILULAN
NARROW	Sah-lah-keh ree-jee-yah dah bah-yah	TSALLAKE RIJIYA DA BAYA
NATIONALITY	Kah-sah	KASA
NATIVE	Eh-nee kah-sah	ENE KASA
NEAR	Koo-sah dah	KUSA DA
NECK	Woo-yah	WUYA
NECKLACE	Sar-cah	SARKA
NEGOTIATE	Tah-tah-oo-nah	TATTAUNA
NEGRO	Bah-car fah-tah	BA'KAR FATA
NET	Ha-she-fah	ASHIFTA
NEVER	Bah	BA
NEW	Sah-bon bah	SABON BA
NO	Wah-nee	WANI
NUDE	Zeen-dear	ZINDIR
NURSE	Jee-yah-tah	JIYYATA

O		
OAK	He-tah-cen (oak)	ITACEN OAK
OATH	Rant-sar dah	RANTSAR DA
OBSERVE	Loo-rah	LURA
OCEAN	Teh-koo	TEKU
ONION	Al-bah-sah	ALBASA
ONLY	Ka-why	KAWAI
OPEN	Boo-day	BUDE
ORACLE	Jah-wah-been-sah	JAWABINSA
OWE	Kam-moo	KAMMU
OWL	Moo-jah-yar	MUJAYAR
OWNER	My	MAI
OX	Sah-nee-yah	SANIYA
P		
PAD	Ah-koo-mah-reen	AKUMARIN
PADDLE	Fee-lah-fee-lee	FILAFILI
PAGAN	Are-nee-yar	ARNIYAR
PALM OIL	Ah-lye-yah-deen	ALAYYADIN
PALM WINE	Bah-meen	BAMMIN
PANIC	Rah-zah-nah	RAZANA
PARCEL	Koon-shun	KUNSHAN
PARDON	Yah-feh	YAFE
PASSENGER	Fah-seen-jan	FASINJAN
PASSING	Woo-say	WUCE
PASSION	Gah-gah-roo-mar	GAGARUMAR
PAWPAW	Kah-boo-shi	KABUSHI
PAY	Bee-yah	BIYA
PEACE	Zah-man lah-fee-yah	ZAMAN LAFIYA
PEEL	Bah-reh	BARE
PENALTY	Fah-nah-reh-tee	FANARETI
PEOPLE	Moo-tah-neh	MUTANE
PERIOD	Mood-dee	MUDDI

HAUSA

PHARMACY	Fahr-mah-see	FARMASI
PIG	Ah-lah-dee	ALADE
PIONEER	Soo-kah kah-sun-say doh-meen-sah	SUKA KASANCE DOMINSA
PITY	Khi	KAI
PLACE	Woo-ree	WURI
POLE	Kwang-wah-lah	KWANGWALA
POLICE	Yan san-dah	'YAN SANDA
POLICE STATION	Cah-gee-r-fee-shin	CAJIOFISIN
POST OFFICE	Fah-sah oh-fas	FASA'OFAS
PRAY	Ah-doo-ah	ADDU'A
PRIDE	Fah-ha-reen	FAHARIN
PRIVILEGE	Gah-tar	GATAR
PROFIT	Ree-bah	RIBA
PSALM	Zah-boo-rahn	ZABURAN
PUMKIN	Kah-beh-wah	KABEWA
PURSE	Lah-lee-tan	LALITAN
PUS	Dee-wah	DIWA
PUT	Sah	SA
PYTHON	Ah-neen	ANIN
Q		
QUAIL	Bar-wunh	BARWAN
QUAY	Ka-wah-tah	KWATA
QUEEN	Sah-rah-oo-nee-yah	SARAUNIYA
QUEST	Neh-mam mah-kee-yah-yah ka-why	NEMAM MAKIYAYA KAWAI
QUICK	He-yah	IYA
QUICKLY	Sun-koo-tah	SUNKUTA
QUILT	Man-zan-neen	MANZANNIN
QUOTE	Sah-koo-reh	TSAKURE

R		
RABBIT	Ag-wah-dah	AGWADA
RACE	Kah-bee-lah	KABILA
RACKET	Dee-dem dee-dem	DIDIM-DIDIM
RADIANCE	Has-ken	HASKEN
RAGE	Koo-lay	KULE
RAIDER	Dan ha-reem	DAN HARIM
RAIN	Roo-wan sah-mah	RUWAN SAMA
RAINBOW	Mas-ha-roo-wah	MASHARUWA
RAM	Sah-sah-jeh	TSATTSAGE
RAMADAN	Ah-zoo-mee	AZUMI
RANDOM	Fee-toe bar-kah-tye	FITO BARKATAI
RANK	Gah-rod	GARAD
RAT	Beh-rah	'BERA
RATE	Yah-wan	YAWAN
RECESS	Loon-goon	LUNGUN
RECIPE	He-rin-sah bah	IRINSA BA
REVEAL	Ban-kah-dah	BANKADA
ROOM	Dah-kee	DAKI
ROUND	Tah-gee-yar	TAGIYAR
RUST	Sah-sun	TSATSAN
S		
SAD	Bah-keen see-kee	BAKIN CIKI
SAME	Ha-kah	HAKA
SAFE	Lah-fee-yah	LAFIYA
SALE	Sah-yar-wah	SAYARWA
SAVAGE	Dan-yen khi	DANYEN KAI
SCHOOL	Mah-kah-ran-tah	MAKARANTA
SCREEN	Ah-low	ALLO
SECRET	Boh-boh-yeh	BOBBOYE
SENIOR	Bah-ban	BABBAN
SENSELESS	Mah-rah-sah	MARASA

SERMON	Hoo-doo-ban	HUDUBAN
SHEEP	Too-mah-kee	TUMAKI
SHOE	Tah-kal- mee	TAKALMI
SHORT	Goon-too-war	GUNTUWAR
SHOUT	So-wan	SOWAN
SHRINE	Ga dah-keen he-hoo	GA ƊAKIN IHU
SIBLING	Sha-kee-kin	SHAKIKIN
SISTER	He-tah say yar-oo-wah-tah	ITA CE 'YAR'UWATA
SMALL	Kan-kan-say	KANKANCE
SON	Dan kah-rah-meen	ƊAN KARAMIN
STATION	Tah-shar	TASHAR
STAY	Koo-zah-oo-nah	KU ZAUNA
STORE	Ah-dah-nah	ADANA
STREET	Tee-tee	TITI
SUITCASE	Fan-tee-moh-tee	FANTIMOTI
SWEET	Koo-noon	KUNUN
SWORD	Tah-ko-bee	TAKOBI
SYSTEM	Sah-reen	TSARIN
T		
TABLE	Kah-woe	KAWO
TALE	He-kah-yah	HIKAYA
TAKE	Cah-he	KAI
TALL	San-kam	SANKAM
TARGET	Bah-rah-tah	BĀRATA
TAXI	Ah-cah-bah	ACABA
TEACH	Ko-yar dah	KOYAR DA
TELEPHONE	Wah-yah	WAYA
TEST	Gwah-jeen	GWAJIN
THAT	Dah	DA
THANKS	Go-diyah	GODIYA
THEOLOGY	He-lee-meen ah-dee-nee	ILIMIN ADDINI

THEORY	Rye	RAI
THESE	Wah-dah-nan	WAƊANNAN
THEY	Ah-kan	AKAN
THIEF	Bah-rah-woe	ƁARAWO
THIGH	Sin-yon	CINYAN
TIDY	Keen-sah	KINTSA
TIGER	Seen-ah-koo-war-tah	TSINAKUWARTA
TIME	Low-kah-cee	LOKACI
TITLE	Kah-noon	KANUN
TODAY	Yow	YAU
TONE	Mye	MAI
TOO	He-kon	IKON
TRAIN	Jur-gen	JIRGIN
TRAIN STATION	Tah-shar jur-gen	TASHAR JIRGIN
TRANSLATION	Fah-sah-rar	FASSARAR
TRANSLATOR	Mah-fah-sah-reen	MAFASSARIN
TRAVEL	Tah-fee-yar dah	TAFIYAR DA
TRUTH	Gah-ski-yah	GASKIYA
TURKEY	Tur-kee-yar	TURKIYAR
TWIN	Tah-gwa-yeh	TAGWAYE
TYPE	Tah-ree-feh-tah	TARIFETA
U		
UDDER	Han-sar	HANTSAR
UGLY	Moo-moo-nah	MUMMUNA
UMBRELLA	Lye-mah	LAIMA
UNCUT	Bah-wan oo-ban-gee-jee	BAWAN UBANGIJI
UNIVERSITY	Jah-mee-ar	JAMI'AR
UTTERLY	Say zah-lah	CE ZALLA

V		
VAGABOND	Dan dan-dee	Ɗan DANDI
VAGINA	Far-jeen	FARJIN
VANISH	Lah-yah-say	LAYACE
VARIETY	Na-hoo-ee	NAU'I
VERY	Dah	DA
VICTORY	Nah-sah-rah	NASARA
VILLAGE	Kah-oo-yeh	ƘAUYE
VIOLENT	Mye	MAI
W		
WAGE	Goo-dah-nar	GUDANAR
WAGON	Wah-goo-noo	WAGUNU
WALK	Tah-fee-yah	TAFIYA
WARRIOR	Sah-dah-oo-keen	SADAUKIN
WARY	He-noo-war-sah	INUWARSA
WASTE	Bah-gah-jan	BAGAJAN
WATER	Roo-wah	RUWA
WEED	Bah-foo-ree	BAFURI
WELL	Dah	DA
WET	Dah-moo-nah	DAMUNA
WHEREVER	Ah dook inn dah	A DUK INDA
WHICH	Dah	DA
WHITE	Fah-ree	FARI
WHOLE	Doo-kah	DUKA
WHY	Don-may	DON ME
WIRE	Wah-yah	WAYA
WISDOM	He-kee-mah	HIKIMA
WOMAN	Tah	TA
WOMB	Moo-sah-man	MUSAMMAN
WORRY	Gah-lah-bah	GALLABA
WRONG	Lah-ee-fee	LAIFI

TALK NIGERIA

Y		
YAM	Ah-nee-gee	ANIGE
YE	Ann-ah-been-sah	ANNABINSA
YEAR	She-kah-rah	SHEKARA
YES	He	I
YOU	Kah	KA
YOUTH	Sah-mar-tah-kar	SAMARTAKAR
Z		
ZEAL	Ah-nee-yah	ANIYA
ZERO	Sah-fah-ree	SAFARI
ZIGZAG	Wan-dar wan-dar	WANDAR-WANDAR

References

1. "Nigeria". Wikipedia. July 19, 2010 <http://en.wikipedia.org/wiki/Nigeria#Demographics>.

2. Martin, Carrie. "Hausa". Minnesota State University. July 20, 2110 <http://www.mnsu.edu/emuseum/cultural/oldworl d/africa/hausa.html>.

3. "Yoruba language, alphabet, and pronunciation". Omniglot writing sytems and languages of the world. July 19, 2010 <http://www.omniglot.com/writing/yoruba.htm>.

4. "Igbo". Every Culture. July 19, 2010 <http://www.everyculture.com/wc/Mauritania-to-Nigeria/Igbo.html>.

5. " Learn Igbo". Igbo Focus Publication. July 19, 2010 <http://www.igbofocus.co.uk/html/learn_igbo.html>.

6. "Counting Of Numbers - Ordinal & Cardinal". Teach Yourself Hausa. July 20, 2010 < http://www.teachyourselfhausa.com/counting-of-numbers.php>.

7. O., Boomie. "Languages and Intro". Teach Yourself Hausa. July 20, 2010 <http://www.motherlandnigeria.com/languages.ht ml#Yoruba>.

8. Awde, Nicholas, and Onyekachi Wambu. Igbo-English English- Igbo Dictionary and Phrasebook. New York: Hippocrene Books, Inc. 1999. Print

About the Author

King Yeotan was born in Lagos Nigeria. He was raised by his mother and father and completed all of his primary schooling as a young boy in his hometown of Lagos. He went on to complete a bachelor's degree in Christian Counseling at Life Christian University as well as obtaining a Bachelors degree in Business Administration. He has resided in the United States for over 23 years. His inspiration for writing this book also stems from a high affinity for the different languages of the world.